MW01285474

DEAD-END LOVERS

DEAD-END LOVERS

How to Avoid Them and Find True Intimacy

Nina W. Brown

 PRAEGER

Westport, Connecticut
London

Library of Congress Cataloging-in-Publication Data

Brown, Nina W.
Dead-end lovers : how to avoid them and find true intimacy / Nina W. Brown.
   p. cm.
  Includes bibliographical references and index.
  ISBN: 978–0–313–35596–7 (alk. paper)
  1. Intimacy (Psychology).   2. Man-woman relationships.
  I. Title.
  BF575.I5B76   2008
  646.7′7–dc22   2008010127

British Library Cataloguing in Publication Data is available.

Library of Congress Catalog Card Number: 2008010127
ISBN: 978–0–313–35596–7

First published in 2008

Praeger Publishers, 88 Post Road West, Westport, CT 06881
An imprint of Greenwood Publishing Group, Inc.
www.praeger.com

Printed in the United States of America

The paper used in this book complies with the
Permanent Paper Standard issued by the National
Information Standards Organization (Z39.48–1984).

10 9 8 7 6 5 4 3 2 1

This book is dedicated to all the men and women everywhere who have yet to find a suitable lover and obtain a meaningful, satisfying, and enduring intimate relationship. I wish you luck.

CONTENTS

Preface   ix

Acknowledgments   xi

1. What Is a Meaningful Relationship, and How Do I Get One?   1

2. Unproductive Relationships and Dead-End Lovers   16

3. Clear Signs of Unsuitability   29

4. The Helper and the Hurting and Needy Lover   45

5. The Saver and the Risk-Taking and Rebellious Unsuitable
    Lover   60

6. The Believer, and the Charming and Manipulative Unsuitable
    Lover   74

7. The Mirror and the Self-Absorbed Unsuitable Lover   90

8. The Curious Rebel and the Exotic, Different, Unsuitable Lover   105

9. Reduce Susceptibility and Build Resistance   119

10. Increase Your Interpersonal Effectiveness   135

11. Become a Winner and Choose Winners   152

Bibliography   167

Index   169

PREFACE

This book describes unsuitable lovers of both genders, the behaviors and attitudes that are troubling to relationships, and some reasons why you continue to be attracted to them. These are not the lovers who just don't work out, both parties recognize this, and break up with some regrets. The relationships meant by the term "dead-end" are those where you end up feeling used, emotionally abused and fragile, wondering how you could have been so foolish as to hook up with this person, feel betrayed and/or rejected, and other such negative feelings. You may wonder why you keep getting into intimate relationships that don't have potential for real intimacy, what kind of lover you are looking for that you haven't found to date, and how to go about finding that person and having a meaningful and satisfying love relationship. These are issues and concerns that are common when someone has had a succession of dead-end lovers.

You can stop picking dead-end lovers when you better understand what you find alluring about them, build your self to have more resistance to these types of lovers, know the signs of unsuitability early in the relationship, and work to become a person who wants and attracts a lover suitable for a deep and enduring relationship. These are some of the topics covered in this book that can get you started.

I want to encourage you to read the material and to work through the exercises. The exercises are designed to get you thinking about your particular situation and your relationships, both current and past. This kind of self-exploration and self-reflection increases your understanding of yourself and of others. You can learn to resist the lures of unsuitable lovers and to recognize signs of unsuitability, and this leads to a reduction or elimination of getting involved with dead-end lovers. You really can stop picking dead-end lovers, and even better, start getting the kind of intimate relationship you've dreamed of having.

ACKNOWLEDGMENTS

No book is written in isolation. There are people who provide encouragement, listen to your ideas and thoughts, give you ideas and thoughts, attend to the technical aspects, and are supportive in many ways. I had many such people while I was writing this book and I want to convey my thanks for their assistance.

Thanks goes first to Radha Parker, my friend and colleague at the university, who gave me the idea for this book when she asked me to substitute for her and present on the topic. That request gave me an opportunity to research why people feel they keep picking losers (I changed this designation). I would also like to thank Debora Carvalko, the acquisitions editor at Praeger, and to the two graduate assistants who worked with me on the book, Lindsay Meyers and Betty Davis.

People who provided encouragement are too many for me to list them all. But, I do want to mention members of my family: my husband Wil; children Toni, Mike, and Linda; and grandchildren Billy, Joey, Samantha, Chris, Nick, and Emma. Thanks for being there.

1

WHAT IS A MEANINGFUL RELATIONSHIP, AND HOW DO I GET ONE?

Gina is a bright young woman working as a waitress in an upscale restaurant while attending a local community college where she is learning to be a computer technician. She has had a number of relationships that went nowhere, and the current one is headed in the same direction. Gina wants to get married someday and is ready for a long-term loving relationship that leads to that. She has become very discouraged about finding the "right" person.

Stuart is an account executive in his mid thirties who has always pictured himself as settling down one day with a family. He has had numerous girlfriends since he was 16, and a few serious ones after finishing college at 22. However, he has not found the woman he could settle down with and have a family. He wonders why the women he's fallen for to date turn out to be unsuitable. For example, he really loved Caroline, but she was into cocaine, a fact that she managed to hide from him for a long time. He only found out by accident when he came upon her snorting some in the kitchen where they lived. When he met Janis, he was captured by her intelligence and vitality. They spent a lot of time together and he started to feel that this relationship had potential. Janis was looking for a job but hadn't found the right one, so Stuart loaned her money to help pay the bills. After six months of this, Stuart finally realized that Janis was not seeking a job, nor did she have any intention of paying back the loans.

Gina and Stuart are two of many examples of people in relationships with dead-end lovers, and who continue to repeat their mistakes in the choices they make. They are not alone as many can relate to the complaint, "Why do I keep picking losers?"

This book is intended to explore that complaint, to help you understand the dead-end lover's attraction for you so that you can take steps to reduce or eliminate these attractions, to help you define what your personal meaningful and satisfying relationship would be, to suggest strategies to build your inner confidence and self, and to present some identifiers for suitable lovers or "winners."

Let's begin with an understanding of the lover you seek.

Exercise 1.1. What Am I Looking For?

Materials: Two sheets of paper, a pen or pencil, and a quiet place to reflect and write where you will not be disturbed.
Procedure:

1. Write the following on a sheet of paper:

   Weather
   Music
   Color
   Book (category, such as mystery, biography, nonfiction)
   An article of clothing
   A piece of furniture
   Food

2. Close your eyes, try to empty your mind, and think about the lover you want. Do not edit or change what emerges, just let it come. If a picture of a real person appears, go with that picture.
3. When you feel you have the picture you want, open your eyes and write a response that reflects or describes the person you are seeking, or the real person that emerged, for each of the concepts you listed on the paper. For example, hold the picture in your mind and write a color that describes or that comes to mind as you think about the picture or the person.
4. You'll now have a list like the following:

   Rainy and windy
   Opera arias
   Dark blue
   Biography of a historical figure
   Shirt—buttondown oxford weave
   Recliner
   Bacon and eggs

Review your list, and make an association for each word. For example, rainy and windy could have an association with the word(s) edge, unexpected, or dangerous. Opera arias could be associated with the work, dramatic. Let the associations emerge quickly without thinking or trying to change them.

5. Once you have your associations, look at them and write a brief description of the person you're looking for. This can be revealing of your nonconscious perception for the person you're really looking for as a lover.
6. (Optional) Try the same procedure for a current, former, or potential lover, and determine how close he/she is or was to your ideal lover.

Put the description(s) in a safe place so that you can review them again as you read the book, and complete other exercises.

Now that you have a more conscious picture of your ideal lover, let's describe a meaningful, satisfying, and loving relationship. Such a relationship would have the following elements:

- Mutual respect and acceptance
- Respect for each other's psychological boundaries
- Empathy
- Fun playfulness counterbalanced with dependability and responsibility
- Trust
- Openness in emotional expression
- Encouragement and support
- Excitement and interest together with a quiet pleasure in each other's company
- Inclusive, not exclusive
- Concern for each other's welfare and well-being
- A lack of blaming, criticisms, and put-downs
- Separateness as individuals

MUTUAL RESPECT AND ACCEPTANCE

Respect for each other as unique, worthwhile, and valued individuals is basic for a loving relationship. You want to feel cherished, as if you matter, that you are significant and important in his/her life, and you give the same in return. Let's do a short exercise about a current or former relationship.

Exercise 1.2. Valuing

Procedure:

1. Reflect on a current or former relationship, use a scale of 1–10 where 1 indicates little or none and 10 indicates considerable, and rate the extent to which you valued that person. Now, rate the extent to which you felt valued by him/her.
2. Was there a disconnect between the two ratings where your rating was much higher than the other person's rating? Or, did you have a low rating for valuing the other person? If so, it may be that you did, or do not, feel valued. Or, you do not value the other person.

Acceptance, like respect, is focused on the person as he/she is, not as you want him/her to be, or if he/she were to change. Does this person accept you as you are, or are there demands or hints that you should change to please him/her? Acceptance as you are does not mean you cannot or should not change some behaviors. For example, if neatness is important to him/her, and you tend not to be neat, you may want to try to be neater as long as the demand for neatness is not excessive.

I once saw a poster for a play titled, "I love you just the way you are. Now, change." That title captures some of what usually happens. You fall in love, the person seems wonderful, but you try to get him/her to change to meet your needs or perceptions. You may even make some changes yourself, or resist changing. However, acceptance of the whole person is very important for sustainability of the relationship. Both of you will change, but changes should be voluntary, not imposed.

Exercise 1.3. Acceptance

Procedure:

1. Reflect on a current relationship that you value. Rate the extent to which you are fully accepting of the person using the previous scale of 1–10, where 1 is "he/she would be ok if he/she did or did not do the following"; and 10 means that you don't see anything that warrants changing.
2. After you complete the ranking, reverse the process and rank how much that person is expecting, demanding, or imposing changes on you.

RESPECT FOR EACH OTHER'S PSYCHOLOGICAL BOUNDARIES

Psychological boundaries can be difficult to describe or explain, but they are the defining points or lines where you end and the other person begins. Physical boundaries are so much easier to describe, but violation of these can also violate another person's psychological boundary. It doesn't help that each person's psychological boundary may be different. Let's look at some physical boundary violations that may also be violating the person's psychological boundary.

- Touching without permission
- Using someone's possessions without asking permission
- Entering someone's room or office without first knocking
- Making a critical comment about someone's physical appearance to him/her
- Giving orders and expecting these to be promptly obeyed
- Making commitments for another person without checking with him/her first
- Telling someone what he/she ought to do or should do
- Giving unsolicited advice

You may want to reflect on which of these you do and how often you do them, and if your current and/or former lover did (does) any of these.

What are the messages that the described actions communicate about recognition and respect for the receiver as a separate and valued person? The person committing these violations is sending the following messages.

- I am entitled to do or say this, and you should recognize my rights and not object.
- I can do or say what I want to because I am right and others should be accepting of this.
- I know what's best or right for you.
- My needs or wants should receive priority from you.
- You need me to tell you what to do, or to organize your life.
- You'd be in a mess if it wasn't for me.
- I don't recognize your space, belongings, or anything as off-limits for me. I can use these at my convenience.
- What's yours is mine at any time I choose.

These and other such messages reveal underlying and possibly unconscious attitudes of grandiosity, arrogance, contempt, entitlement, and other such self-absorbed behaviors and attitudes. The psychological boundaries between self and others is not clearly defined for this person, and others are perceived as extensions of one's self and under the self's control. So, when these people violate other's physical and psychological boundaries, they may not recognize that they are doing so, and in some cases, the people may not care that they are violating these. They are convinced that they are superior and have a right to do what they are doing. The reasons for these attitudes and behaviors are complex, and if you want to understand the self-absorption you can read information on narcissism. Two books that address self-absorption are *Children of the Self-absorbed* (Brown, 2000) and *Loving the Self-absorbed* (Brown, 2003).

But, back to respecting each other's psychological boundaries. In addition to not, or seldom, doing any of the actions in the list, or seeming to have these attitudes, your lover and you should have and/or do the following:

- Allow each other to have separate opinions and ideas without feeling let down, wrong, or betrayed. Do not expect or push for agreement for opinions and ideas.
- Use courtesy and civility in interactions. Say please, thank you, and ask permission when appropriate
- No shoving, pushing, hitting, or other such actions even as playful love taps.
- Refrain from advice-giving. Find out what the other person wants to do, correct misinformation, provide needed information, help explore alternatives, but don't tell the other person what he/she should or ought to do.
- Give compliments and refrain from criticism. Develop ways to sensitively give suggestions for improvements, but always recognize that these are your perspectives and that the other person does not have to agree.
- Let others speak for themselves.
- Don't ask intrusive questions, or ask so many questions that it feels like an interrogation, or put him/her in a position where he/she feels that he/she cannot have any private thoughts, or that he/she has to account for every minute out of your presence. Some measure of trust in the relationship is helpful.

EMPATHY

Empathy is a wonderful experience where the person feels fully understood. It is also a rare experience. Some people equate empathy with sympathy, or in becoming overwhelmed or enmeshed in someone's feelings, but these states are not what is meant by empathy. These are cognitive responses in the case of sympathy, and lack of boundary strength for the other two. Empathy occurs when you can sense the inner experiencing of the other person, tune in to what is being felt *without* losing your sense of yourself as being separate and distinct from him/her. You are not left with residual feelings that you are unable to let go of as what happens with becoming overwhelmed or enmeshed.

That said, empathy is very important for a meaningful, satisfying, and loving relationship, and should be reciprocal. You must both give and receive empathy, and not have this as one sided in the relationship. It is not necessary to be always empathetic, but it is important to be frequently empathetic.

Do not confuse empathy with agreement. Just because someone understands what you are feeling does not mean that he/she agrees with your feeling or the rationale. For example, suppose you are angry and hurt at a remark made by a friend. Your lover can empathize with your anger and hurt, but can still retain enough separation and individuation not to agree that the remark was insensitive, just that it did appear that way to you. Countless fights and disagreements have resulted from an expectation that empathy meant agreement, and when that was not forthcoming, the person became angry because of the lack of agreement, and/or felt that if the person really loved them and understood how he/she felt, then the person would agree with him/her.

Empathy is a gift that makes you feel understood at a deep level, and that you are valued. It is this empathy and unconditional positive regard that, when received as an infant and as a child, provides the basic foundation for a strong and cohesive self. As adults, the ability to be empathic is associated with the many positive traits of healthy adult narcissism, and is enriching to your relationships.

Reflect on a time when you felt you received empathy from another person. You probably felt relief that someone attended to you enough to pick up on your feelings, you felt that the person was sensitive and caring, you were comforted that you were not alone at that moment, and you felt encouraged and supported. These are the kind of feelings that help validate the self as worthwhile and valued, and that build strong connections. It can be very important for you and your lover to be empathetic with each other.

FUN AND RESPONSIBILITY

An element of fun and playfulness enlivens any meaningful relationship. But, unless that is counterbalanced with responsibility on the part of both parties in an intimate relationship, then one party has to assume all or most of the responsibility. This situation can lead to developing negative feelings where one person is focused on play and fun, and the other person keeps trying to get him/her to recognize and accept their responsibilities.

Fun and play bring out some child-like qualities that can be endearing and can arouse one's delight and wonder. Both of you want the other to enjoy and participate in each other's version of fun and play. Take a moment to reflect on your version of fun and play by completing the following exercise.

Exercise 1.4. Fun and Play

Materials: several sheets of paper and a pen or pencil for writing.
Procedure:

1. List 8–10 activities you think are fun and playful on one sheet of paper.
2. For each activity, identify if it is a solitary activity, a cooperative activity, or if it needs a group or a mass of people to be completed. An example of the latter is a party.
3. On a separate sheet of paper, make a list of the cooperative fun and playful activities derived from your first list.
4. Next, identify the feelings aroused in you when participating in each cooperative activity, and the approximate date when you last participated in it.
5. Look at this list with its associated feelings and dates. Do you have a very few such activities, or numerous ones? Did you participate recently, or has considerable time passed since you did that activity? Does your partner think these are fun?
6. The final part of the exercise is to take a new sheet of paper and make a list of the activities your partner thinks are fun. Compare these with your list in Step 5. How many of them are similar? Are there any on your partner's list that you do together? Are there several activities he/she likes that you either don't like, or don't want to do? Which list is the longest? Do you find that you frequently participate in activities just to please him/her?

Adult responsibilities are many, and there are times when they can appear to be overwhelming, and you wish you had fewer, or that you could get away for a while. However, you probably just keep on trying to meet your responsibilities even if there is carping, complaining, and other acts that reveal your feelings about your plight. Think about your current lover or spouse. Does he/she meet his/her responsibilities most of the time? Or, is this person mostly focused on pleasure, fun, play, and the like? If the latter is the case, then fun and play is not counterbalanced with responsibility. If he/she tends to be overly responsible with little or no fun and play, then the other counterbalance is lacking. Dead-end lovers tend to have the former more than the latter.

TRUST

Some people end up in more than one relationship with a dead-end lover because they inappropriately trust others. It can seem sometimes, that, regardless of negative experiences such as betrayal, they rush back to bestowing their trust in someone rather than reflecting on their deep need to trust, and working through their feelings of betrayal.

Trust is a bedrock for meaningful, satisfying, and enduring relationships. Trust usually involves the following:

- You believe that the person cares for you.
- He/she has concern for your welfare, is open and truthful, understands, values, and cherishes you.
- He/she wants the same relationship that you do, is committed to the relationship, and wants it to grow, develop, and endure.
- He/she will not mislead you or push you to do things you do not want to do.
- He/she is not out to exploit you for his/her advantage.

Does this describe you in a relationship? You may want to take some time to reflect on your past relationships and recall some of your feelings, attitudes, motives, and so on about him/her to see if you had acted in accord with the description. If you have failed relationships that involved betrayal of trust, then you may want to reflect on what you are seeking that allows you to overlook or ignore signs of betrayal or lack of trustworthiness. Yes, the other person acted badly, but you wanted the relationship so much that you did not take care of yourself, and it could be helpful to better understand your motives.

It may be that your life experiences to this point have caused you to be wary, suspicious, and cautious in relationships, and you may be hypervigilant to the possibility of betrayal. You've been betrayed and misled enough that it is difficult for you to trust. This is what you've learned from your experiences, and you are in a mindset designed to protect yourself from being further betrayed and hurt. You may even have tried to put your suspicions and apprehensions aside and have trusted another person who then also betrayed you, leading you to berate yourself for making that mistake again. All of these experiences can make it difficult to let go and trust once again. However, a relationship without trust cannot be meaningful and satisfying, and so you are caught in a dilemma. If you want a loving and meaningful relationship, you'll have to have trust in the other person, but your experiences have not predisposed you to trust, and you don't have any or much faith that your trust would not be misplaced or abused.

Let's propose that trust be perceived as something to be earned for both of you. Your lover has to earn your trust, and you have to earn his/hers. Trust is developed over time with the following actions:

- No lies for convenience, to placate, or to prevent distress
- Open admission of mistakes, errors, and the like

- Keeping promises, and not making promises that cannot be kept, or that there is no intention of keeping them
- Being dependable and reliable
- Not making critical comments about others who are absent
- Not deliberately making misleading statements
- Show faith and belief in the other person until there is reason to be otherwise

OPEN AND HONEST EMOTIONAL EXPRESSION

An open emotional expressiveness can be very helpful in a relationship so that you do not have to guess what the other person is feeling, especially when that feeling is important for the relationship. This is not to say that either of you must express every fleeting thought and feeling as that could become tiresome to have to do and/or to listen all of the time. Trying to guess feelings can also lead to mistakes that can then make the person feel misunderstood, and that too is eroding for the relationship. Both of you can help strengthen the relationship with open and honest expressions of your emotions.

Not everyone can be open and honest in expressing their emotions, mainly because of family of origin experiences and expectations where expression was not encouraged and/or it was punished. People growing up under those conditions learned to suppress their feelings so well that they may not be able to access these as they are now repressed. Some people may not be open and honest as they are trying hard to win acceptance and approval, and fear that they will be rejected if their real feelings are openly expressed. Neither of these contributes to a healthy and positive relationship.

This is not to suggest that some tact and politeness are not used. There can be times when it is *not* helpful to openly express your feelings, such as the following:

- When the other person's emotions are so intense that whatever you say could be misunderstood
- When the other person is upset and may not be able to accurately hear you
- When you may be meeting your needs at the expense of the other person
- In a public setting when you or the other person can become embarrassed or shamed
- As a put-down, demeaning, or devaluing of the other person
- To try and force the other person to do something he/she does not want to do, or is not in his/her best interest

Trying to guess what someone is feeling can be very frustrating, even when you know the person very well as there are occasions when what is felt or experienced is hidden or masked. Strong relationships are usually those where both partners are willing to be open in their emotional expressions and aware of the impact of these on the other person. Both are important for the relationship because the other person may not be in a state or place where he/she can hear and understand your feelings, or vice-versa.

The important thing for a relationship is that each person be sensitive to the other person but, at the same time, be willing and capable of open expression of their important feelings.

ENCOURAGEMENT AND SUPPORT

A major part of showing caring and concern can be found in the degree and kind of encouragement and support provided. These can be subtle, such as just being there, or overt, such as speaking words that point out one's strengths. Both are tailored to the individual and what is perceived as encouraging and supportive for one person may not be so for another person.

Reflect on your most positive relationship to date, and let yourself remember how you felt being with that person, and how he/she encouraged and supported you. What words were used that encouraged you? What actions did he/she take? Now, reflect on your current relationships to see how or if these provided you with encouragement and support. You may find that there are one or more persons that you view as encouraging and supportive, and these are the relationships that are most meaningful and satisfying that can also be cultivated to be enduring.

On the other side, you may also want to reflect on the extent to which you give encouragement and support to the others in your relationships, and/or if you know what they perceive as encouraging and supportive. There may be some room for improvement on your part.

Don't use encouragement and support with compliments and flattery. These can be pleasing to receive, and some may even be sincere and realistic, but are not what is meant by encouragement and support. In significant and important relationships, encouragement and support has the following characteristics:

- It is genuine and heartfelt
- Attention is given to the needs of the receiver
- Sensitivity to the other person's emotional state, and even empathy are provided
- Words are carefully chosen to convey intent
- Logical and reasonable, not illogical and/or unreasonable
- Are not used to manipulate and control

EXCITEMENT, INTEREST, AND QUIET PLEASURE

Intimate, meaningful, satisfying relationships usually have some measure of excitement and interest on the part of both persons. There is energy that seems to increase when you are together, and a void when you are apart. You may even feel that something is missing when you are not together. Interest in each other is also present and can be a part of the excitement. You want to know more about the person because you like him/her, and you want him/her to know more about you and to like you in return. That unfolding and discovery can lead to forming stronger and enduring bonds.

A relationship where there is one-sided interest and excitement, or where there is only sexual excitement is not usually meaningful or sustainable. Once the initial flush dies down, there seems to be nothing left that keeps the people together, and it is helpful to stay aware of the transitory nature of these relationships. If the interest is one-sided, you may want to ask yourself why you are interested in someone who is not interested in you, or where you are providing your own excitement as the other person is not excited about you. You are likely to find that you are wasting your time, and that he/she does not and will not have the excitement and interest that a mutually constructive one provides.

Some indices of excitement and interest on your part can be the following:

- An increase of energy when you are with him/her
- A delight in what he/she says and does
- You desire to know some important things such as his/her hopes, dreams, plans for the future, and the like
- Your values and principles seem to be similar
- You are sensitive to his/her emotions and moods, but don't become enmeshed or overwhelmed by these
- You like him/her

In addition to the excitement and interest, there needs to be a quiet pleasure in each other's company, where each is relaxed, open, genuine, and accepting. Theses states can be the basis for developing trust and safety for a relationship, and their value should not be underestimated. It can be tiring to live in a spiritual state of excitement, and your body and mind can suffer the effects of stress. After all, not all excitement is pleasurable; some excitements come from fear and other unpleasant emotions. The body reacts in the same way for pleasant and unpleasant, and stress results. So, while some excitement is energizing and pleasurable, you still need to provide some down time for the system to recover. This is one reason why a positive relationship has both energy and quiet.

Quiet pleasure can be felt in situations like the following:

- Fond smiles for each other without words
- Not having to fill silence, feel the need to chatter, or having to be going or doing something all of the time
- Listening with interest
- Engaging in activities where you work cooperatively
- Taking a stroll, hike, bike ride, or something similar where you are aware, but not having to fill silences

Your nonverbal behavior signals a liking and pleasure for his/her presence. Your comfort level is such that you can let your real self be seen, and this is reciprocal.

INCLUSION, NOT EXCLUSION

Both of you come to the relationship with a set of previous relationships, and this new one does not exclude the old ones, nor is it a barrier to forming other new relationships. Yes, your time and energy will be organized and directed differently, but this relationship should include these other relationships, and not exclude them.

Love expands the self, and the more you can love, the more you are enriched. For example, the addition of a child to a family can expand their love to include this child. Everything changes, but everything is richer for this inclusion.

Your lover, spouse, or partner is very important to you, but that should not mean that you must love your family and friends less. It is best when it means that you have expanded your heart and self to love more. Love should not mean possessiveness, mistrust of others, jealousy, and other such negative states and feelings. These do not enrich a relationship; they isolate and alienate you from a rich source of love, encouragement, and support.

This is not to say that you continue to give these other relationships the same priority that they held earlier. There will be some significant changes in the amount of time and effort devoted to these relationships. If this love relationship is to endure, it must receive priority much of the time, and the major part of your time and energy. Emergency situations, of course, are the exceptions. The bottom line is that you want to expand, enrich, and enhance your life through your relationships.

CONCERN

Concern and caring for each other's welfare is an important consideration when building a relationship you want to endure. Notice that this care and concern is not one way; it includes both parties. The ideal relationship is one where the other person's welfare is of utmost importance, and where you are willing to take care of him/her, to be supportive and encouraging, to persist through the dark and uncomfortable times, to let his/her needs be more important than yours when necessary but not all of the time, to be sensitive to unspoken needs for acceptance and approval from you, and to be as nonjudgmental as possible.

You don't have to always agree with him/her, or to take over and take charge when he/she can take care of himself/herself, or to be overly concerned. Both of you are separate and distinct adult individuals and this should not be forgotten. Concern for his/her welfare does have limits, and these limits should be kept in mind so that you don't go overboard. Care and concern is not shown by doing things that you feel are not in your best interests; violate your values or principles; are unethical, immoral, or illegal; demean you in some way. Nor should you expect any of these from the other person. You do not have to demean or devalue your self to show care and concern for someone's well being.

- Ask about them rather than dwelling on what's happening with you
- Be willing to listen to their problems and concerns without trying to fix these
- Learn to recognize and be sensitive to their moods
- Take what they say seriously, and don't minimize this to try and lighten the mood
- Appropriately see to their physical comfort

LACK BLAME, CRITICISM, AND PUT-DOWNS

This phrase is very descriptive of how a relationship becomes meaningful and satisfying because each person in the relationship refrains from blame, criticism, and put-downs. Just reflect for a moment on your most unsatisfying relationships and recall how these acts contribute to the dissatisfaction. It is likely that these relationships experience one or more of these acts that are eroding one's self-esteem and thereby eroding to the relationship. Also reflect on your tendencies to do any of these, and what the impact is on others. I think you will find they do not strengthen the relationship nor do they help with meaning and satisfaction.

If you are the target for one or more of these acts, you may be experiencing the following, none of which are helpful for a relationship:

- Shame for having fatal flaws that are visible to others, and which can never be fixed
- Guilt for not living up to your and/or others' expectations
- Inadequate and not good enough
- Anger as the charge is a threat to the visibility of the self
- A desire for revenge, to hurt that person as you've been hurt
- A sense of their superiority, and of your inferiority
- Denial and resistance to the charges
- Feeling that you are being treated unfairly
- Wanting to flee and hide

More positive for a relationship is for both to accept each other, to not demand perfection, or expect mind reading, to not project or displace personal dissatisfaction on the other person, and to care about each other enough to be sensitive to his/her needs.

SEPARATE INDIVIDUALS

Relationships fare better when each person has developed to the point where the personal concept of being a separate and distinct individual is deeply understood. This development begins in childhood, and may continue throughout one's life. Some people lag in their development, and do not gain, or fully gain, this deep understanding. Not understanding this concept of being separate and distinct from others can lead to boundary violations, becoming enmeshed, and/or a tendency to allow oneself to be exploited or to expect others to let you exploit them. None of these are positive for relationships.

Some indices of understanding include the following:

- Respect for others' privacy, possessions, and the like
- Not making assumptions about others' needs, desires, and wishes
- Allowing the other person to speak for himself/herself, volunteer his/her time or effort, and so on
- Accepting differences of opinion, and so on, not demanding total agreement with you
- Able to tolerate diverse perspectives, activities, and the like
- Liking him/her as he/she is, and not demanding that he/she live up to a fantasy or ideal
- Not needing to control him/her

WORKING YOUR WAY THROUGH THIS BOOK

The remaining ten chapters are intended to provide you with enough information about yourself and your tendencies to be attracted to dead-end lovers so that you can make more informed choices about intimate relationships. This journey begins with a description of meaningful intimate relationships so that you have a goal in mind as to what such a relationship should be. This also gives you some notions about where your current and/or former relationships are/were lacking. The remainder of the book should trigger your thinking about how to get and maintain the kind of intimate relationship that is affirming, satisfying, deep, and enduring.

Chapter 2 focuses on unproductive romantic relationships and describes how you can get sucked into these. You have lures that are unconscious, related to your experiences in family and other relationships, your personality, and the circumstances or situations where you interact with others. You will be helped to identify your lures.

There are clear signs that some lovers are unsuitable, but you may not be aware of what these are, or you may minimize or ignore these. You may not have thought of behaviors and attitudes that signal that this person is unsuitable because of their lack of responsibility, self-absorbed behaviors and attitudes, troubling emotional and psychological unresolved issues, and illegal behavior. Chapter 3 presents and describes these clear signs of unsuitability, and gives an overview of five types of unsuitable lovers.

Chapters 4–8 goes into more detail about each type, the attraction they hold for you, and how you can start monitoring your thoughts, feelings, and behavior to become more resistant to the lure of the unsuitable lover. The exercises and reflections are also contributors to building your self to become more centered and grounded, have stronger psychological boundaries, reduce emotional susceptibility, and other such growth and change factors.

Chapters 9–11 focus on building your self. Chapter 9 presents thought-provoking exercises to help you understand your emotional susceptibilities, and presents strategies to reduce these. Chapter 10 describes how to increase your interpersonal effectiveness by understanding and monitoring your unconscious nonverbal behavior, learning to be a more effective listener and give more understanding responses, and reducing your self-absorbed behaviors and attitudes. Chapter 11 finishes the process with a review of how far you have come in your journey to understand why you tend to pick dead-end lovers, presents strategies designed to help you make better choices for intimate relationships, and makes suggestions for further growth and development.

2

Unproductive Relationships and Dead-End Lovers

Few people enter a relationship expecting that it will be unproductive. There is an excitement and eagerness about the potential for the new relationship and many hopes, dreams, and fantasies. The realization that the relationship is unproductive and not at all what is wanted or envisioned gradually emerges over time. Even when there was a defining incident as a series of events that produced this realization, there were disquieting signs along the way that were minimized or ignored. This chapter presents four phases for relationships that are unproductive and unsettling, some tips on how you can recognize what is happening on a more conscious level, and what can be alluring to you that forms the basis for your continuing to choose dead-end lovers. The four phases are romantic illusions, edges appear, disillusionment, and sorrow termination.

Romantic Illusions—Phase 1

Although romantic illusion will differ from person to person, and especially between men and women, the basic feelings and perceptions will be the same, and this is what is presented here. Don't forget, there are two words, and the other is illusion where objective reality is ignored or minimized. It has no place or role during this phase, which can carry the feelings of bliss, happiness, excitement, and lust. There is no wonder that people seek this state when it can produce these feelings. Even after several negative experiences, the positive aspects can seem so rewarding that you seek to find it over and over again. Let's do an exercise to clarify what you consider to be romantic in the beginning stage of an intimate relationship.

Exercise 2.1. Romance

Materials: Several sheets of paper, a pen or pencil, and a set of colored pencils, felt markers, or crayons.
Procedure:

1. Find a place to work with a table or other firm surface for writing and drawing.
2. Sit in silence with your eyes closed, and allow a picture of romance to emerge. Pay attention to the details of the picture and to the feelings you experience as you think about romance. If several pictures emerge, select one that seems most pleasurable or focal.
3. When you have your picture and feelings selected, open your eyes and draw the picture. (Artistic talent is not required for the exercise. Put as many details in the picture as you can, and when you are finished, give your picture a title.)
4. Next, take a clean sheet of paper and list the feelings that emerged as you thought about romance. If other feelings emerged as you drew the picture, also list these. Select a different color for each feeling and draw a symbol for that feeling. For example, if excitement is one of your feelings you could select a bright yellow and draw a spray of yellow lines similar to a firecracker explosion. Use one color for each feeling.
5. The final step is to review what you drew and the list of feelings.

Now write a summary paragraph about how you perceive romance. Try to answer the following questions in your summary:

What seems to be the most important to me?
What are the most intense feelings? These are the feelings where you selected the strongest, deepest, or brightest colors for your symbols.
How might my perception of romance be misleading me?

Now that you have a firmer idea of what romantic means to you, let's take a look at illusion as it relates to romance. Read this cinquain and see if it captures some of what you define as illusion.

Illusion
Blurs edges
Misty, calming, affirming
Cannot see anything clearly
Misleading

Romantic illusion is a part of what is often called "seeing the world through rose-colored glasses," wherein the person only sees the positive, good, desirable, and pleasurable aspects, and either refuses to see the opposite or puts a positive spin on the ugly or negative aspects. The illusion that all is wonderful can be powerful and difficult to relinquish, even in the face of mounting evidence to the contrary. You may want to understand your tendency toward romantic illusion by completing the following scale.

Exercise 2.2. Illusion Tendency Scale

Directions: Rate yourself on the items using the following scale.

5: Very much like me, or almost always
4: Much like me, or often
3: Somewhat like me, or sometimes
2: Occasionally or seldom like me
1: Not at all like me, or almost never

 1. I try to see the good in everyone regardless of what they do or say.
 2. I am sometimes exploited or taken advantage of because of my good nature.
 3. I go out of my way to take care of others often at the expense of my own needs.
 4. I seek others' approval.
 5. I get upset when others seem to dislike me or not approve of me.
 6. I am shocked when others behave badly, or are inappropriate in some way.
 7. I easily forgive others when they do or say something hurtful or disparaging of me.
 8. I expect others to be as accepting and respectful as I try to be.
 9. I expect others to be truthful.
10. I prefer "white lies" to the brutal truth at times.

Add your ratings to obtain a total score.

Scoring: Scores will range from 10 to 50. Scores of 41–50 indicate that you are highly attached to illusion and it plays a significant role in how you perceive and relate to others. Scores of 31–40 indicate that you use considerable illusion in your perceiving and relating. Scores of 21–30 indicate that illusion plays an important role in your perceptions and relating, but that you are able to be realistic at times. Scores of 11–20 indicate that illusion does not play a significant role in your perceptions and relating, but that there are times when it does come into play. Scores of 5–10 indicate that you seldom, if ever, allow illusion to influence your perceptions and relating.

You may want to reflect on the role that romantic illusion plays in your continuing to select unsuitable, or dead-end lovers, and why the fantasy is so attractive. Use the items in the scale that you rated 3 or above as a guide for what you may want to consider changing so that you reduce your susceptibility to romantic illusions. This inner personal development is explored more in later chapters.

EDGES APPEAR—PHASE 2

Now, every relationship that goes on for any length of time starts to settle down. The excitement wanes and wanes, but is still present in sufficient quantities to be thrilling. But what happens in an unproductive relationship is that you have moments of disquiet where something seems off-key, but you cannot identify what is producing the disquiet, or the disquiet may remain just below the level of consciousness where you are experiencing it, but are not consciously aware. The just below your awareness disquiet may be reflected in your attitude, words, or actions. For example, you object to something about the person, become cranky and rationalize that you may be coming down with something, or that you had a bad day. You both dismiss it as a blip in the wonderful relationship and soon forget about what had happened. But, the disquiet remains and grows, or you firmly repress and deny that you have such feelings. Even if you were to admit to yourself that you had these feelings, you would be hard pressed to identify what caused them.

Mostly, you just ignore these disquieting feelings. You can also begin to experience some disappointment about the person. He/she does not appear to be as perfect as you once thought. However, when you become disappointed in or with someone, you need to take care that the disappointment is not because of your self-absorbed attitudes such as an entitlement attitude, excessive attention and admiration needs, a lack of empathy on your part, and/or grandiosity. Your disappointment stems from the other persons failure to line up to the principles and standards and values you thought he/she had and lived by. Examples of events, actions, and attitudes that may be disappointing include the following:

- Insensitivity to you and/or others
- You feel manipulated to do something you do not want to do, or that you feel is wrong
- He/she asks you to lie for him/her
- He/she asks you to do something illegal
- More focused on his/her needs and ignores yours
- Often criticizes you
- Blames you for his/her mistakes
- Uses intimidation tactics, or tries to arouse your guilt
- Is not reliable
- Cannot depend on his/her doing what he/she agreed to do

You may discount the importance or significance of your disappointment in an effort to retain the feelings experienced in phase 1, and mostly these positive feelings are retained. You can have some moments of thoughtful reflection about the disappointments, but you can easily dismiss these, blame yourself for being too picky or too demanding, or other such rationalizations.

The most troubling acts that signal the appearance of edges are his/her lies, distortions, and misleading statements. There are many reasons for the lies and the rest, but these have no place in a genuine and loving relationship. There are numerous reasons for lies, but all have the goal of deception, even white lies. Let's start off with theses socially acceptable lies that almost everyone has used at one time or the other.

- If a friend were to ask you if his new hair cut or style was becoming or flattering, and you do not think so, would you say "no"?
- When someone asks you how you are doing and you have several distressing life events going on, would you reply with something like, "Rotten"?
- You attend a play that was awful. Afterward, the mother of one of the actors asks you if you enjoyed the play, would you say, "No"?

- Your spouse or girlfriend asks you if her dress makes her look fat, would you reply, "You betcha"?

My hunch is that you would be less than fully truthful in all or almost all instances like these. Your rationales would be something like the following:

- I don't want to hurt his/her feelings.
- I don't want to be rude.
- No one really wants to hear about my life.
- I don't want to offend anyone.
- He/she might get upset.

All rationales for the white lies focus on you, not the other person. You don't want to have to deal with the fallout or outcomes you imagine will happen. You are protecting yourself from fantasized unpleasantness. It seems much easier and smoother for the relationship for you to tell a "white lie" that many think is harmless.

The rationales for telling white lies are also the rationales for telling more substantial lies, and this is one of the things that happens with the dead-end lover. He/she uses the excuses that he/she doesn't want to be rude, offend, get you upset, and so on. This person rationalizes that he/she is just trying to keep the relationship smooth, and that what you don't know won't hurt or upset you, that ignorance is bliss. There are other reasons for his/her lies such as exploitation and manipulation. However, in phase 2 you are unlikely to recognize these lies for what they really are, be unaware of the impact of these on you and on the relationship, and easily accept his/her rationalizations for "white lies." Your rose-colored glasses are firmly in place.

Even though you have some disquieting feelings on occasion, these are not troubling, and you can easily dismiss them or explain them away. However, they do have an effect as some of the intensity of feelings experienced in phase 1 diminish to the point where you can feel the difference. Instead of viewing this as a necessary condition for transitioning to a deeper and more meaningful level of connection, you try to regain that intensity. You can even find that you are declining yourself about the intensity of your feelings in an effort to keep the excitement at a high level.

What can be happening is that your unconscious disquiet is trying to seep through your conscious, but you firmly repress and deny this. If you were to become aware, accept your disquiet, reflect on it, and examine it, you would lose the pleasant intense feelings and the relationship. Since you perceive this person as your dream lover, you are not about to do anything to lose him/her. The extent to which you can go to retain and/or reclaim the pleasant intense feelings experienced in phase 1 can be considerable and extreme. You may find that you are doing all or many of the following:

- Compromising your principles
- Not acting in accord with your values
- Doing unwanted things in order to retain his/her interest

- Trying too hard to please him/her, and not succeeding as much as you formerly did
- Feeling anxious and upset without really understanding why you feel this way
- Displacing negative feelings on friends, colleagues, family, and even strangers
- Worrying a great deal about potential loss of the relationship
- Ignoring signs of deception and/or betrayal
- Allowing yourself to be exploited and/or manipulated

The other thing you may notice, but minimize, is that you are the only one making an effort to recapture the intense pleasurable feelings from phase 1. Your lover seems receptive, but does not initiate action or dialogue. However, you are not yet at a point where you are able or willing to admit or accept that you are putting most of the energy into the relationship. This phase can continue for some time because you repress, deny, rationalize, and minimize any reservations you have about the relationship.

DISILLUSIONMENT—PHASE 3

The mist of your illusions begins to dissipate and some unpleasant realities intrude on your happiness. You start to see what you have not let yourself see clearly.

- There are constant and deep disappointments
- A noticeable lessening of attention on his/her part
- You are fed up but cannot let go
- You keep giving him/her one more chance
- You experience considerable hurt, anger, and resentment

Your psychological self that was developed through a combination of personality, family or origin experiences, and positive and negative experiences in other relationships will determine what constitutes deep disappointment for you. For example, you may be deeply disappointed when your partner forgets a special day for you like anniversary or birthday. Or, you may not think of these as special days so you are not disappointed when you don't receive gifts or other recognitions. However, most people will be deeply disappointed when their partners do the following:

- Fail to keep promises, or agreements
- Take another person's side in an argument, or a disagreement, especially in public
- Are overly affectionate with someone else
- Do not want to be with them during trying circumstances or through adversity
- Lie, cheat, distort, and mislead
- Do and say things designed to erode their self-esteem

At one time you were able to ignore or rationalize some of these, but they happen so often that you cannot overlook them any longer, or be unaware of the impact on you.

The next exercise can be difficult to do, but it could help you clarify your feelings about a current relationship, or make visible some things that would help you in the future to recognize a dead-end lover early in the relationship. Do as much or as little as you choose.

Exercise 2.3. Disappointments

Materials: Several sheets of paper, a pen or pencil, and a set of felt markers, crayons, or colored pencils
Procedure:

1. Find a place to work where you will not be disturbed. Sit in silence and recall the course of the relationship with a current lover or spouse, or with a former lover you think is a dead-end lover.
2. As you recall events, thoughts, and feelings, write down any that were deep disappointments for you. You may have minimized or ignored them at the time, accepted the explanation or apology, but the initial feeling was one of deep disappointment for you.
3. Select a color for each item you wrote, and draw a symbol or shape on another sheet of paper. This symbol or shape should capture the essence and intensity of that particular deep disappointment.
4. When you complete your drawings, take a close look at what you wrote and drew. Use another sheet of paper and write a paragraph about both that begins with, "As I look at this depiction of my disappointments, I am aware_____."
5. Keep your writing and drawing with the exercises and scales you completed previously.

The disillusionment phase can also bring with it an awareness that your partner's attention has noticeably lessened. Where before he/she listened to what you had to say, he/she now seems distracted, bored, and not very interested. What you may be picking up on are some nonverbal signs of disinterest or inattentiveness such as the following:

- Looks directly at you less often when you are talking
- Does not orient his/her body toward you
- Changes the subject abruptly or without notice
- Starts talking over you about his/her concerns
- Interrupts you
- Is looking around almost always when you are out, e.g., party, restaurant
- Doesn't look out for your comfort, needs, and the like
- Is not available as much as he/she was previously

There are many ways to be less attentive, and these describe only some of them. Further, each person can differ in the need for attention, how attention is conveyed and displayed, and in their definition for a noticeable lessening.

It would not be unusual for there to be some lessening of attention in a relationship as there is usually some decrease in feelings, and partners become more comfortable with each other to the extent that they still feel connected and that the relationship is safe even when attention strays, other events intervene, or each of you does his/her own thing. Nor does it mean that you have excessive attention needs where you expect your partner to give you all of his/her attention most of the time. What is meant here is that you are aware of receiving less of your partner's attention, you are sensing a signal of disengagement, and you are uneasy about the strength and endurance for the relationship.

What can be distressing in the long run and final analysis is that you may try harder and harder to recapture the attention, but you are not fully successful. You may use negative tactics such as demands, tears, attacks, and the like. These usually have the effect of driving the person further away and of producing shame, hurt, and other negative feelings for you. When you look back at this time in the relationship, you can be appalled at your lack of awareness and the efforts you made to try and keep or to recapture this attention.

At some point you may become fed up with what you are doing to try and preserve the relationship, and with your partner's attitude and behavior, but you *cannot let it go*. Every time you think about ending the relationship, you start to panic and back off. You convince yourself that the preservation of the relationship is worth your time and effort, that you are wrong about the extent of his/her commitment to you and to the relationship, and the thought of being out of the relationship is very scary. This is what is known as ambivalence. You, at the same time, see the constructive aspects for you of staying in the relationship, and see the destructive aspects. You become stuck, mired, and paralyzed. You cannot let go the relationship. Try the following exercise to better understand what you may be experiencing.

Exercise 2.4. Letting Go

Materials: Several sheets of paper, a pen or pencil, and a set of crayons, felt markers, or colored pencils.
Procedure:

1. Find a place to work where you will not be distracted or disturbed. Sit in silence for a few minutes to clear your mind. When you are ready to focus on a current or former relationship where you experience or experienced some disillusionment. Recall your many experiences, feelings, and thoughts.
2. Write a list of the feelings and thoughts about yourself, the other person, and the relationship. Don't edit your list, evaluate or rationalize the thoughts and feelings, just list all that emerge. Write as many things as you wish, but try to have a minimum of ten to fifteen items.
3. Read your list and select the one thought or feeling that seems most significant or important to you at this time. Then select a color(s) that reflect the feeling

or thought and draw a symbol, an abstraction or just a splash of color to
reflect that thought or feeling.

4. Under your depiction of the thought or feeling, write a sentence that explains
   its importance to you, what is the thought or feeling saying about you, the
   other person, and the relationship.
5. Select the next three most important thoughts and feelings, and repeat steps
   3 and 4.
6. Finally, write a summary paragraph about your four drawings and statements.

This summary could focus on what you are thinking and feeling that is making
it difficult for you to let go of an unproductive relationship.

Your deep needs and desires can lead you to hanging on and giving the
dead-end lover "one more chance" countless times. That one more chance
becomes several, time passes, you are not free to explore yourself in other
relationships, your dissatisfaction mounts, you exaggerate anything you believe
is positive or that seems a beginning of change, and you don't know why you
keep hanging on. You may rationalize the negative actions that keep you
disquieted, make excuses to yourself and to other people, keep the hope alive
that he/she will become more like what you thought they were at the beginning
of the relationship, believe the lies that are designed to tap into your needs
and insecurities, and may even pat yourself on the back for being so generous
and willing to provide another chance.

Now, there are times when a relationship or person deserves another
chance, or even more than one. But, these are situations where you can
see some visible indicators for change, or trying to change. Examples of these
could be similar to the following:

- The partner spends considerably more time with you rather than with his/her
  friends
- He/she makes some attempts to change the behavior(s) that are most distressing
  to you after you verbalize clearly what these are
- There is concrete evidence that he/she has a job, and can support him-
  self/herself over a long period
- Debts to others are paid
- You are not expected to provide financial resources
- Behaviors become more dependable and responsible

You probably can think of more examples where there is evidence that
the person is sincerely trying to change, and it would not be foolish to give
him/her another chance. These circumstances are different from those with a
dead-end lover. With the dead-end lover you have to accept that they are not
going to change, you cannot make or cause them to change, and you don't
need to continue to try and fool yourself that he/she will change, especially
after you've provided them with one or more chances to demonstrate changes.
You need to reflect on how many "one more chance(s)" you've given him/her

and ask yourself, "How realistic is it to expect that he/she will change given his/her history with me to date?" Let your initial reaction guide you to the answers.

We've only briefly touched on the feelings that you experience during this phase. Let's do a short exercise to clarify what feelings you are experiencing.

Exercise 2.5. Phase 3 Feelings

Materials: A sheet of paper and a pen or pencil.
Procedure: Find a place to work where you will not be disturbed.

1. Close your eyes and let your thoughts go to your partner and the relationship. Focus on all the feelings that spontaneously arise as you think about these. Do not edit or change them, just let them come into your awareness. When you are ready, open your eyes and complete the remaining steps. Following is a list of some feelings you may be experiencing. Select all that apply, and add any you wish to get a list of at least ten feelings.

Anger	Shame	Excitement	Pleasure
Fear	Guilt	Surprise	Happy
Resentment	Anxiety	Calm	Sad
Disappointment	Stuck	Restless	Remorseful
Peaceful	Panic	Rage	Humiliated

2. After you have your list of ten or more feelings, review the list, and write a sentence about each as it relates to the relationship.
3. Review your sentences and write a summary paragraph using the words and sentences as your guide. Put this with your other materials.

If you have more negative than positive feelings, or more intensely negative feelings, you are probably well into phase 3 of this relationship.

SORROW TERMINATION—PHASE 4

This phase can be hard on you and on everyone around you. You are displeased with your partner, yourself, and life in general, and the tendency to displace your feelings on others can be considerable. You don't like anything or anyone. You've reached a decision, but you don't yet want to act on it, and when you do act on it, you can begin to second guess your judgment. Phase 4 is characterized by intense uncomfortable negative feelings accompanied by defenses to preserve your self. Some common feelings that are experienced are:

- Regret
- Shame/disgust
- Guilt
- Relief
- Depression
- Despair

Regret emerges from the ending of a relationship that began with such promise for you. Shame and/or disgust that you allowed yourself to be fooled and misled, maybe even doing so once again, and you wonder why you keep doing this. Shame emerges at thoughts and feelings of not being good enough to keep away from making the same mistake, not being attracted to "winners," not seeing the person as he/she really is, and maybe even that you cannot be fixed so that you do not make this same mistake again. This shame goes to the core of your essential self, and provides a deep narcissistic wound.

There can also be guilt for acts you did that did not live up to your values, principles, and standards. Guilt emerges when you think and feel that you were manipulated and exploited into doing foolish things, or things that you did not want to do, and that now you regret that you were not strong enough to resist.

Along with regret, shame and guilt can also be feelings of relief. Relief that a decision has been made for better or worse, and that you no longer feel stuck in an unsatisfactory relationship. You are moving out and moving on to something new. This relief can feel like a load being reduced or lifted, allowing you to think, feel, and act as you once did. You are not chiding or berating yourself for staying with a dead-end lover, wondering why you cannot let go, and reducing many of the other feelings experienced in phases 3 and 4.

Some people may experience depression and despair. It would be unusual not to have some sadness about the loss of what started out as a promising relationship. Then too, the relationship may have dragged on for some time, and the inability to change it or to let it go can produce some feelings of depression. Some people can be despairing of ever finding a suitable partner, of continuing to select dead-end lovers, and about their ability to fix themselves to attract someone who can relate to them in a more positive way. There are many complex and complicated feelings that can be experienced in phase 4, and it can take some time to work through these. In effect, you are mourning the loss of a relationship, even though it was not satisfying.

Why are you attracted to dead-end lovers? If you are reading this book, you have probably experienced more than one dead-end lover where you invested time, energy, passion, other inner parts of your self, and material resources, but he/she did not adequately reciprocate. You may be wondering why you are attracted to this type of person even when you make an effort to analyze the attraction so as to avoid making the same mistake, but it also turns out to be a dead-end. What can be happening is the magic of lures.

Lures are your internal states, wishes, desires, needs, and fantasies that get activated by something about the other person. Until you understand your lures better, you will not be able to consciously and unconsciously resist these, and can continue to be attracted to dead-end lovers. The remainder of the book describes some types of dead-end lovers, their attraction for you, and how you can fortify your self to resist the attraction. Briefly presented here are six categories of lures: fun, physical attractiveness, excitement, rescuing, romance, and exotic. Use the following scale to determine your preferential lure.

Exercise 2.6. My Lures Scale

Directions: Answer each of the items using the following scale.

5: Extremely attractive to me, I really like this
4: Very attractive to me, I like this
3: Attractive to me
2: Attractive sometimes
1: Not at all attractive to me; I do not like this

1. Provides frequent opportunities to play.
2. I want to feel carefree and not weighed down with responsibilities.
3. Makes me laugh a lot.
4. Not stuck in a routine.
5. I enjoy playing games with others very much and frequently.
6. Beautiful/sexy people get lots of attention and admiration.
7. I'd like to be seen with a glamorous TV or movie star.
8. I fantasize about being with someone famous.
9. Attractive, glamorous, and famous people lead fantastic lives full of romance.
10. Attractive people are powerful and tend to get what they want.
11. Risk-takers, adventurous people are very exciting and attractive.
12. I want someone who does extraordinary things.
13. When I am with someone who is adventurous and takes risks, I get energized and excited.
14. It is important to me to feel unique and special so I seek partners and lovers who make me feel this way.
15. "Bad boys or girls" are not ordinary, mundane or conventional, and associating with them gives me a thrill.
16. I want to make the difference in my lover's life.
17. It makes me feel good and powerful when I can give advice, provide solutions, help make decision that "fixes it" for the other person.
18. I have a strong need to be needed by my lover.
19. I really believe that I can save someone from doing something that is self-destructive or harmful.
20. I like it when someone listens to me and does what I tell him/her to do.
21. It feels so romantic to have someone give me his/her full attention, listen to what I say, and be really interested in me.
22. I want my lover to plan romantic times for us.
23. Teasing and playing hard to get are my ways of showing interest and building excitement.
24. I feel special and valued when my lover does romantic things and that puts me in a good mood.
25. It is very important that I always, or almost always, please others.
26. It energizes and excites me when I meet or interact with someone who is from another country, ethnic group, or is vastly different from my usual contacts.
27. I like to be seen with a lover who is visibly different from me.
28. It is a challenge that is exciting to try to get to know a lover from a different background than mine.

29. Exotic or different people have an undefinable quality about them that I find very attractive.
30. I like the attention and the feeling of being unique and special when I am with someone exotic or different.

Scoring: Add your ratings for the following clusters of items.

1–5 ——
6–10 ——
11–15 ——
16–20 ——
21–25 ——
26–30 ——

The highest possible score for any cluster is 25. Note your highest score(s) and use the following as a guide to your lures.

1–5: The lure is fun. You like the idea of being carefree, happy, and not having to deal with problems or responsibilities.

6–10: The lure is physical attractiveness. You tend to romanticize and glamorize those you think are handsome/beautiful. You like to be seen with them and enjoy the reflected attention, admiration, and even the envy.

11–15: The lure is excitement, risk-taking, or even danger. You find this to be energizing and being with someone like this expands your concept of your self and what you can do.

16–20: The lure is rescuing. You have strong nurturing needs that can lead you to believe that you need to take care of others who are, or should be, taking care of themselves.

21–25: The lures are seduction and romance. You play hard to get, and are attracted by others who also play hard to get. You value and seek romance and romantic gestures.

26–30: The lure is exotic and different. You long to get away from the conventional, usual, and what you think is boring. You may even expect that someone who is exotic or different has answers for you.

Even when you understand what is alluring for you, it can be difficult or impossible for you to resist the lure. You may even already know what lures you to a dead-end lover, but succumb to it every time. We'll discuss these lures, how to recognize when they are causing you to lean toward making an unwise decision, and provide suggestions for how you can stop yourself. But, before we explore the lures, we take a look at some clear and visible signs of unsuitability in Chapter 3.

3

CLEAR SIGNS OF UNSUITABILITY

Chapter 1 presented some characteristics of meaningful relationships, and Chapter 2 described the course of a relationship that is a dead-end. The challenge is to recognize the signs in advance that the potential relationship can either be meaningful or will become a dead-end with all of the emotional fallout that is so negative for you. This chapter begins the process for guiding you to stop entering unproductive and dead-end relationships, and to develop meaningful and satisfying relationships by achieving an understanding of the clear and unambiguous signs of unsuitability. Also presented are some of the more subtle behaviors and attitudes that generally signal unsuitability, a way of categorizing types of unsuitable lovers, and a beginning for understanding why you can be attracted to the unsuitable lovers. This chapter focuses on topics that are further defined, described, and elaborated on in subsequent chapters.

Central to the presentations are the following objectives:

- Building your awareness of your self factors that predispose you to the attraction
- Understanding your unconscious needs, desires, and fantasies for intimacy and intimate relationships
- Identifying areas of your self that have not yet been fully developed, and the roles that these can play in your attraction to unsuitable lovers
- Accepting that the other person cannot be changed by your efforts. Any changes must come from within that person, and not from what you do, say, want, demand, and so on
- Making a realistic appraisal of your idealized image of the lover you seek
- Preventing your romantic illusions from blinding you to the clear or subtle signs of unsuitability

SIGNS OF UNSUITABILITY

Carolyn was so angry with herself, and could not stop thinking that she must be the dumbest woman in the world. "Why can't I stop making the same mistake, over and over again," she thought. "I should have known that he was no good, that I was wasting my time, that he didn't care for me, but no- o- o, I had to hang on until he rejected me in front of everyone. What's the matter with me?"

Carolyn is an example of someone who is attracted to an unsuitable lover, doesn't understand why she is attracted, and ends up hurt and rejected in every one of the relationships. There are numerous external signs or indicators that suggest that a person is unsuitable for an intimate relationship, and many of that person's internal characteristics are visible from the person's words and actions such as an entitlement attitude. Following are two lists, behaviors and attitudes, of characteristics that are usually associated with people who lack the capacity to form and maintain satisfying and enduring relationships. You may think that your relationship with the person will be different and more positive, but an examination of your past relationships is likely to reveal that you have used that faulty thinking before, with very unsatisfactory results. Review the lists and determine if any of these describes a current or former intimate partner, if there is a pattern of characteristics to which you are attracted, and reflect on how you may have rationalized, denied, or ignored some signs of unsuitability.

Behaviors

Behaviors can be observed, but attitudes are inferred, and inferences are subject to unconscious error. However, the attitudes listed are usually visible from the person's words and actions over a period of time, not just from one event. These may not have been directed at you, but don't make the mistake of thinking that you are immune, that he/she would never do that to you, or other such magical thinking.

The behaviors can signal emotional and mental instability that is deep, enduring, and can/has negatively impacted the quality of life and the person's relationships. You will be taking on a daunting and impossible task to try and change the person, or to make him/her want to change. Change is possible under the right circumstances, such as adequate mental health treatment, but providing what is needed is out of your range of competence. Just think about it, professional treatment does not work all of the time, requires education and training, and requires some level of cooperation from the person. You are unlikely to have the expertise needed, and to be blinded by your emotional involvement. In addition, the person probably sees no need to change, or does not have the will and discipline to change, and your efforts will generally end up as futile. The following list gives examples of behaviors that signal unsuitability, and a brief definition or description of what is meant.

Deadbeat mom or dad—does not assume financial responsibility for his/her children

Irresponsible mom or dad—has children by several different partners, does not marry any of them, and does not support the children

Sex addict, convicted sex offender, and/or extreme interest in pornography
Confused about his/her sexual identity—has multiple partners of both sexes
Does not provide any personal information—secretive and uninformative
Difficulty in managing anger—frequent and irrational outbursts of anger
Physically violent to you and others
Delusional and/or other signs of mental or emotional instability
Characteristic life pattern of self-destructive behavior—frequent run-ins with the
   law, school dropout, unable to establish and maintain meaningful relationships
Sexual predator—uses sex as a weapon, to control and/or to exert power
Has a history of "using" others to get what he/she wants, to gain an advantage,
   to manipulate and control
Can be explosive at times but hides it well
Excessive and uncontrollable gambling
Has no visible means of support that cannot be accounted for by something such
   as a trust fund
Uncontrollable shopping, spending, and so on
Alcohol and/or drug abuse including prescription medicines
A long record of repeated arrests for felonies whether convicted or not

Hidden Acts That Can Signal Unsuitability

You may not know about or recognize some acts as signals of unsuitability because these are hidden or you are unaware of their importance as concerns about character. Among these are

- Numerous arrests for felonies
- Gambling, shopping and other such addictions
- Internet pornography/sex addiction
- Contagious sexual disease that is untreated, or untreatable, e.g., HIV, that is
   kept secret
- Assumption of a false identity to escape creditors or the law
- Mean spirited and vicious

These are behaviors and attitudes that signal a lack of responsibility, denial of self-destructive acts, a desire for revenge for real or imagined injuries, refusal to accept the consequences for personal actions, and an ability to rationalize moral, ethical, and legal transgressions. The personal commitment for these people is likely to be to self, with very little if anything left to give to others that would enrich a relationship.

How can you know if your potential lover has any of these hidden behaviors? You probably don't have an inclination or resources to check for arrests, outstanding warrants, and other criminal system information. Most states do require sex offenders to register as such and these names are available to the public. These are usually available on the Internet through a state or local law enforcement agency. However, multiple arrests and assumption of a false identity can go undetected to all but a very few law enforcement personnel who have the time and resources to find this information, and even then many people go undetected.

You may be cautious about entering a love relationship with someone who does any of the following:

- Refuses to talk about his/her background or changes the subject when this arises
- Has large gaps of time in his/her life that is not accounted for
- Is evasive and secretive about his/her whereabouts, activities, and the like on a regular basis
- Asks you to lie when he/she receives calls or visits from people he/she is evading
- Makes a good or decent salary, but often is broke or frequently borrows money for daily living expenses

Most troubling is that you can't know or detect much about hidden things. Even experts can be misled, especially about addictions that don't bring the person into treatment. I don't have much to offer you here, except that, once you suspect that any of these exist for your lover, you are well advised to get out of the relationship as quickly as possible.

Attitudes

Attitudes can be inferred from verbal comments and other actions, usually as a pattern over a period of time. Some of the following attitudes can be identified by your reactions to what the person does and says. For example, an entitlement attitude could be inferred when someone refuses to wait his/her turn and pushes to the front of the line, or demands preferential treatment. Many of the example attitudes in the list are reflective of undeveloped narcissism where that person does not have a clear understanding that there are other people in the world who are different, but they are also worthwhile. These are your very self-absorbed people whose perspective is always about them, have a pattern of unstable and unsatisfying relationships, and lack appreciation and respect for anyone who is not him/her. These people are unaware of the impact of their behavior on others, and nothing you do or say can make them aware of this. They think that others are the problem and are not shy about letting you know that you are inadequate and wrong.

Feels the world is against him/her, everyone is out to "get" him/her, suspicious of everyone including you, says he/she is persecuted
Arrogant, contemptuous, superior attitude
Feels entitled to be cared for with no personal effort on his/her part
You sense an emptiness or deadness within him/her
Takes pleasure in scamming others
Indifferent to the impact of his/her words and actions on others
Cares more about himself/herself than about anyone else in the world
Hates anyone who is "different"

Now, some of these behaviors and attitudes can be such that there could be an explanation or reason that can allow you to overlook or ignore it as temporary or unusual for that person. Some are more deep-seated and cannot be explained away. Some, like confusion about sexual identity, may be well hidden. Further, there may be numerous positive characteristics about that person that permit you to downplay the negative ones. You may even be aware of some of these, but have the fantasy that the person will change, or he/she says that he/she will change, and you want to believe. The charge that you get from being with the person can blind you to reality as well as some of your personal characteristics, needs, and desires contributing to your blindness. We'll explore most of these throughout the book, but right now the focus is on guiding you to better recognize subtle signs and strong clear signs of unsuitability.

This long list of characteristics, behaviors, and attitudes are just a sample. There are some others that are more definite and clearer, with little or no ambiguity about them. Let's take a look at some of these. Complete the following scale for someone who you found to be unsuitable, and then retake it with a current prospect in mind.

Exercise 3.1. Signs of Unsuitability Scale

Rate the person using the following:

5: Very much so, or extremely like this person, or always or almost always
4: Very much like the person, frequently
3: Somewhat like the person, sometimes
2: Little like the person, seldom, or occasionally
1: Not at all like the person, never or almost never

1. No visible means of support (NVMS)
2. Not seeking employment, education, independence, or the like
3. Borrows money from you and others
4. Expects you to pay for practically everything, including his/her personal expenses
5. Has a criminal record with no signs of rehabilitation, atonement, or remorse
6. Consorts (hangs around) with known criminals and the like
7. Has no realistic aspirations, ambitions, or plans that would lead to a productive life
8. Unreliable and/or not dependable
9. Lies, cheats, distorts, misleads
10. Abuses alcohol and/or drugs
11. Does not respect other's boundaries, takes advantage of others
12. Engages in verbal and/or physical abuse of you and of others
13. You have more lust for the person than you have liking
14. This person is, or seems, angry much of the time
15. Possessive of you, checks on your activities
16. Is actively in another intimate relationship, e.g., marriage

Scoring: Add all of your ratings to obtain a total score, and use the following as a guide for interpreting the score.

61–75: Very clear and unambiguous signs of unsuitability
46–60: Clear and strong signs of unsuitability
31–45: Has numerous behaviors and attitudes that signal unsuitability
16–30: Exhibits many behaviors and attitudes that signal unsuitability
0–15: May have a few such behaviors and attitudes that could signal unsuitability

If you found yourself inclined to think of mitigating circumstances to explain, defend, excuse, or rationalize some described behaviors and attitudes so as to produce a better image and lower rating, you may want to reflect on what you are doing, and what personal purpose it serves. It is important that you be honest with yourself about this person, because keeping an illusion or fantasy about him/her will help you continue to keep relating with unsuitable lovers. Let's examine each of the items on the scale.

No Visible Means of Support (NVMS)

One major assumption for this book is that you and the other person are adults and thus, are expected to have some legitimate means of support. These means can be parental support, a trust fund, or a job. Who or what is the source of funding for your lover's food, shelter, and other basic life necessities? You may want to be very cautious about associating with anyone who does not have any visible signs of support as this lack may suggest criminal activity, or at the very least, a lack of personal responsibility. In any event, this person does not have the basic qualities for suitability as a lover, partner, or spouse. If the person does not have a job or other visible source of income, you will want to see if this is consistent with his/her spending, and possession of material goods, such as cars, televisions, designer clothes, and the like. If there is a disconnect between spending and income, such as driving an expensive car and living in a condo while employed in a minimum wage job, you will want to be just as alert as if the person had NVMS.

Not Seeking Employment

There is the possibility that this person is in transition, and does not have a job at this particular time. There are some valid reasons for a transition state, but the person should be planning and seeking employment, or education to obtain a better job or to enter a career, or to become an independent self-supporting adult. These things do not just drop into your lap, you have to expend some time and effort to obtain them, and a lack of doing so can be a strong signal of unsuitability. If he/she isn't actively seeking employment now, it is likely that he/she will continue on this path, and will not obtain employment, or education, or independence.

Borrows Money

The trouble is not with borrowing money from you and others, unless this action is continual, it's the failure to repay the loan. If he/she cannot manage personal finances now, there is scant or no reason to believe that he/she will be able to do so in the future, and that can produce additional stress for the relationship.

Further, it can be revealing to know what the money is used for as this also provides clues to the person's sense of responsibility, self-discipline, and the ability to care for oneself. Is the money being used for necessities, for alcohol and/or drugs, gambling, to buy nonnecessities, and so on? If the person's necessities are not being met because he/she is spending that money on non-necessities, that is a sign of lack of responsibility that usually extends to other parts of the person's life. The other reasons for borrowing are self-explanatory, and you may want to ask yourself why you are funding these irresponsible and self-destructive behaviors.

You Are Paying

You may be in a relationship where you find yourself paying the lion's share, or for everything including your lover's personal expenses, clothes, rent or mortgage, cars, and so on. There may be a temporary and good reason for this, and you have to judge this. But, if one or both of these are lacking, you may need to consider the possibility that you are being exploited. Is there a valid reason why an adult who wants this relationship cannot secure funds to pay for some part of what is wanted and needed? The important point is that there should be mutual contributions, not necessarily equal, so that the financial burden is shared.

Criminality

Just having a criminal record does not necessarily make the person unsuitable. Mistakes can be made, penalties incurred, and regrets produced. People can and do change. However, if he/she has a sustained criminal record over time, and shows few or no signs of remorse, rehabilitation, or determination to change, you have clear evidence of unsuitability. You may have the fantasy or delusion that you are going to say, do, or be something that will make him/her change. The desire for change comes from within, and you need to wait until you see considerable evidence of positive changes before beginning or remaining in the relationship. It took years for him/her to reach this point or to do those things, and it will take some time before there is behavioral and visible evidence of change.

Consorts with Criminals

Any law enforcement officer, prosecutor, defense attorney, judge, or person who knows something about the criminal justice system will tell you that it is not helpful, wise, or constructive to consort with known criminals, even if you have the best intentions. So if your partner, lover, or spouse hangs out or around with known criminals, this is not a positive sign of suitability. Friends and cronies are very much alike in attitudes, ideas, and much of their behavior, and this can be cause for concern if the companions are unsuitable. Odds are that those who are in close or constant contact with these criminals will absorb some of their attitudes and behavior. Not a good sign.

No Aspirations or Plans

The important concept for this item is the word realistic. Does your partner, lover, or spouse have realistic aspirations and plans for a productive life? Or, are his/her fantasies and unrealistic expectations getting in the way of reality? There is nothing wrong with hoping and dreaming and then working to make these come true. You can dream of wealth, but it takes time and effort to get it (unless you have someone who wills wealth to you). But, mostly, you have to work and strive to achieve and be productive. It is much more helpful and constructive to have realistic aspirations, plans to achieve these, and then work to make it happen.

Unreliable

Trust and safety are built in a relationship when each person is reliable and dependable. Promises are kept, their word is their bond, and only exceptional and unforeseen circumstances are allowed to intervene to keep them from meeting these obligations. If you are in a relationship with someone who is unreliable and undependable, don't expect changes. This behavior works for that person, and he/she sees no reason to change, especially since you remain in the relationship. Nothing you say will make a difference.

Lies, Cheats, Distorts, and Misleads

What can I say? No relationship can be sustained, satisfying, or constructive with constant lies and so on. Nor is it possible that he/she only does these to and with others, but does not do the same with you. The person who constantly lies, cheats, distorts, and misleads does this with everyone, feels justified in putting something over on others and taking advantage, and you are no exception.

You may want to trust him/her, and may have started out doing so only to find that there were many instances of lying, misleading statements, and/or distortion of facts to make him/her look better, be blameless, or to be perceived as superior. The reason(s) for lying are many. You may want to ask yourself how much evidence do you need that someone is not trustworthy, and why are you continuing to try and make the relationship work when it is clear that he/she cannot be trusted.

Alcohol Abuse and/or Drug Use

Abuse of alcohol, such as binge drinking, can signal a serious problem for the person, and help may be needed. However, you are seriously fooling yourself if you think that you can cause a change in the abusive behavior. The person needs expert help that is beyond what you can provide. The same is true for drug use with the added constraint that such use is probably illegal. Until the person accepts that the use and abuse is self-destructive and takes steps to address this, you cannot help and need to realize that this person is unsuitable as he/she is for the present.

No Respect for Boundaries

Boundaries are both physical and psychological. These are the defining points between you and others, that is, where you end and where others begin. Some people do not have a clear sense of being separate and distinct from others, unconsciously think of others as extensions of their self, and thereby do not recognize or respect others' boundaries. Examples for not respecting physical boundaries include acts such as pushing, hitting, or even touching without that person's permission, or taking possessions without asking. Examples of not respecting psychological boundaries include intrusive questions, disparaging and demeaning remarks, and exploitation of other people.

Verbal and/or Physical Abuse

Abuse is not to be tolerated. You do not deserve to be hurt, humiliated, and demeaned. If you are in a relationship where either or both are taking place, do not entertain the fantasy that it is going to stop because it will not. Addressing this problem, or even explaining it adequately, is beyond the scope of this book and I recommend that you consult with experts in domestic abuse for a better understanding and options.

Lust Versus Liking

Lust can prevent you from being realistic about the person and your relationship. You may want to reflect and decide if you like him/her as he/she is. Think about the exhibited behavior and attitudes with you and with others, and if these are illustrative of a person you can like. Notice that I don't say love. It is possible to love someone without liking him/her, but that is usually unlikely. However, it is not unusual to be physically attracted to someone and to not like him/her at the same time. Acting on lust alone is usually not wise, since a meaningful, satisfying, and enduring relationship needs a firmer foundation such as that wrought by liking the person.

Angry

Does this person seem angry much or all of time? Is he/she easily angered, and does not appear to be able to let go of the anger? Does the anger get displaced on you or others? Is the anger so constant that the person is hostile? If your answer to any or all of these is yes, then you are dealing with a potentially explosive person that can lash out unexpectedly and at any time. No positive relationship can exist when you have to be on edge, cautious, and tentative, and/or fearful of saying or doing something that results in arousing his/her anger. You need to know that you do not cause the anger, or make the person angry, as that anger is his/her responsibility and comes from within as a response to a perceived threat. The same is true for you, others do not cause your emotions, you decide what you feel. This is discussed in more detail later in the book. For right now, you just need to know that a constantly angry person is unsuitable for a positive and constructive relationship.

Possessive

Possessiveness of a person is a symptom of insecurity, a feeling or perception of inadequacy, and a fear of abandonment. The possessive person has learned this response through family of origin and other past experiences. The person's fear leads them to relationship destruction actions such as constant monitoring your whereabouts, who you associate with, having to know what you are doing and with whom all of the time, constant phone calls, and other jealous behaviors. You may try reassurance, but that does not work as you can never give enough reassurance so that he/she will not be afraid.

As you read the list of behaviors and characteristics you may be realizing that the unsuitability is not exactly disguised or hidden, you've known this about the person for some time. The challenge now becomes one of understanding why you find enough satisfaction to continue the relationship in the face of evidence, and why you discontinue this relationship, the next one is also apt to be with someone who is unsuitable. Chapter 4 through 8 will explore this attraction in more detail.

Emotional and Physical Abusers

Emotional and physical abuse has been described but you may minimize these behaviors for a variety of reasons. The romantic illusions described in Chapter 2, or incomplete recovery from a former relationship, and/or inadequate self-esteem can be factors in the failure to recognize an abuser. You are so relieved to have someone different from those in previous relationships that you fail to pay adequate attention to the warning signs. Read the following list of behaviors and attitudes to get a better sense of what the warning signs are so that you can take appropriate action to protect yourself. Try to stay open when reading these and don't minimize or rationalize any that are present for the person. There are fourteen behaviors and attitudes, and the person will have most or all of these (Phillips & Phillips, 2007).

- Pushes for quick involvement
- Jealous, especially intense jealousy
- Controlling—interrogates you constantly, keeps the money, wants you to ask permission to go anywhere
- Unrealistic expectations for your use of time, dress, behavior, thoughts, and the like

- Isolation of you from your family and friends
- Blames others for what happens to him/her
- Makes others responsible for his/her feelings
- Hypersensitivity to perceived criticisms, blame and/or abandonment
- Cruelty to animals or children
- Playful use of force during sex
- Rigid gender roles
- Sudden mood swings
- A history of past battering
- Threats of violence to you, for example will say that he/she will break your neck but then turns around and says that he/she didn't really mean it. Take threats of violence seriously.

While all of these are signals, you may be unaware of some of them, he/she may hide some from you, or you may think that they are unimportant, rare or trivial for this relationship. Such thinking can lead you to make unwise choices that you will probably regret in the future. Do not ignore any of these signals, especially cruel behavior to children and/or animals, past battering, playful use of force during sex, and threats of violence. If you are unsure about your interpretations for his/her behavior, or have experienced the emotional and/or physical acts, get in touch with an agency in your community that handles domestic violence. There should be knowledgeable personnel available for consultation and advising. Above all, do not accept emotional and/or physical abuse.

FIVE TYPES OF UNSUITABLE LOVERS

Let's look at five types of unsuitable lovers: hurting and needy, risk-taking and rebellious, charming and manipulative, self-absorbed, and exotic and different. These are not mutually exclusive and you may know someone who has characteristics of more than one. These are categorized as types for ease of discussion.

Just listing characteristics does not give a full picture about the type of unsuitable lover that attracts you. What I mean here is that one of these may be a type that attracts you, but you are not aware of the type, or why that type is alluring for you. The five different types will be briefly described in this chapter and each will be explored in more depth along with some possible personal characteristics that you have that contribute to the allure for you.

Hurting and Needy

This person wears their hurt and neediness on their sleeve, and don't have much difficulty in letting you know that they are hurting and that you can possibly make the difference. Their list of injuries is long, and the perceived injuries are usually legitimate. For example, their families were dysfunctional, they were betrayed, they did experience rejection, and they do have bad luck for some things. It's easy to understand why they are hurting and needy. He/she may wear a facade of self-assurance and competence, and it is only later that you realize how hurting and needy he/she is, that continues to produce the same negative results. In addition, my hope is that you can start to build your self so that you are attracted to lovers who are positive, respectful and appreciative of you, and who wants to develop a meaningful, satisfying, and enduring relationship with you.

Unsuitable lovers who are looking for someone to heal their hurt and fulfill their deep-seated needs fall into this category. They may, or more likely may not, be aware of what they are looking for, but their deepest desire and need is for something that was withheld or not provided from an early age. They don't know what that something is, but they cannot or do not know how to get it for themselves, and are never satisfied with what they do get. It's never enough, and, until they understand themselves better and resolve some of their long-standing and deep issues and concerns, will never be able to get enough. But, this does not stop others from trying to give him/her what is needed although their efforts are in vain.

This lover can be very sweet, attentive, and willing to let you see their vulnerability. You are drawn to this part of them as it fulfills some need or self-perception you have. You want to take care of him/her, and give him/her what was not received in previous relationships. What you probably don't realize is that what this person is missing and yearning for is something that has its roots in the lover's earliest experiences that were injurious to the developing self, and additional experiences have only added to the initial injury. No matter what his/her external persona conveys, internally he/she experiences much of the following:

- Fear of abandonment or destruction
- A sense of inadequacy
- Low self-efficacy—ability to influence what happens to him/her
- Not being good enough to be loved and cherished
- A need for constant validation that he/she exists
- A deep and abiding hurt that cannot be expressed in words

This lover is so impoverished, deprived, and undeveloped that there is nothing to give to anyone else. The acts that convey sweetness and attentiveness are really an attempt to get something to fix the hurt and deprivation, but since these resulted from someone else a long time ago, the people in his/her life along the way could not provide what was needed and wanted, and you will be no different, you will not be able to provide it either.

Can this person ever get what is needed? That possibility exists, but only when the person is willing to do extensive work to develop the self, resolve family of origin issues and concerns, and develop an understanding of self in the world. He/she can heal the hurts, provide for the early deprivation, and become secure enough to be able to enter into a meaningful relationship that does not demand so much from the other person. It is also possible that some of the other characteristics that signal unsuitability are also ameliorated.

Risk-Taking and Rebellious

This lover can exude an air of excitement, energy, and mystery that can be very appealing. You want to know more about him/her and are drawn to the energy and excitement that surrounds him/her, and which seems to be a part of his/her being. You may even become more energized when you are around him/her, and you like how this makes you feel. You are willing to ignore even clear signs of unsuitability to retain this feeling.

This type of unsuitable lover doesn't confine his/her risk-taking and rebelliousness to himself/herself, but can draw you into it, leading you to do things that are not in your best interests, or that are even dangerous. You can get so caught up in the excitement, what you are feeling, and a desire to please him/her that you get carried away and do things that you would not ordinarily do. Others around him/her can become less thoughtful and reflective of the consequences for their actions and start to reflect some of the risk-taking and rebellious behaviors.

This type of unsuitable lover may have experienced a lot of chaos in his/her life where little or nothing was predictable or consistent. He/she could have excessive demands placed on him/her to take care of the emotional welfare of adults in his/her life where his/her emotional needs were ignored, minimized, or neglected. The resulting response was rebellion against those in authority, a defiance against having to do what others wanted, and risk-taking to get revenge and to show off. This is only one possibility, there are others, but the basis for the risky and rebellious behavior was set early in life, the behavior is a way of getting his/her needs met, new experiences and new relationships such as the one he/she has with you will produce lasting changes in the behavior, and the negative consequences suffered or are possibilities, are not a deterrent.

Living life on the edge can be interesting and exciting, but that's where the energy goes into taking chances and avoiding negative consequences. There is scant energy left for developing and maintaining the relationship, growing as a person, or of having a meaningful purpose in life. Bodies and minds are healthier when they can get needed rest. Staying energized and excited does not permit you to get the needed rest, or to be reflective of what you are doing, what needs you have, how to become the person you want to be, or to make your relationships constructive and meaningful.

Charming and Manipulative

Charm is hard to define but the charming person usually has the following qualities:

- Ability to capture your interests
- Makes you feel special and unique

- Gives you lots of attention
- Seems to admire you (or says so)
- Shows interest in you and what you do
- Talks about something that interests you
- Listens as if you are the only person that matters to him/her
- Produces a feeling of well-being in you

Reread this description and you will realize that the focus is mainly on how that person makes you feel, and your feelings can lead you to becoming manipulated. Manipulating others is the main goal for this type of unsuitable lover, and he/she uses your needs and desires to get you to do what he/she wants you to do. You act to get him/her what he/she wants, which is not always best for you.

This type of unsuitable lover can appear to be connected to others but, in reality, is distant and disconnected. He/she has unconscious internal notions that others only exist to serve him/her, that he/she has a right to exploit others, and that others are less worthy than he/she is. Put this attitude together with someone who has inadequate boundary strength, and is needy for external validation of self-worth, and is susceptible to flattery, and it becomes easy to see how the person can become manipulated. Even when you know or feel that you are being manipulated, you may be powerless to stop it because of your unconscious needs that the charming and manipulative unsuitable lover has identified and is using. You are not valued for your self, but only for what you can do or give him/her. When you have nothing left to give or that he/she wants, this type moves on to the next victim. Charm works because of the needs and susceptibility of the receiver, and that is what your task is, to work to understand your needs and take care of these yourself, and to reduce your susceptibility to charm and manipulation. Not an easy task, but a worthwhile one.

Self-Absorbed

It is all about him/her, but he/she is unaware of the impact the behaviors and attitudes on others, and that unawareness can have the most negative impact on the relationship. Others in relationships with the self-absorbed person do not understand that this person is blind to this part of his/her self, and no amount of telling, or any other actions, can make or help him/her see the negative impact on others.

Unsuitable lovers who fall into this type will exhibit most or all of the following characteristics:

- Inflated self—grandiosity, entitlement, arrogance, contempt for others
- Indifference to others—lack of empathy, his/her wants receive priority, has to "win"
- Self-centered actions—boasting, bragging, attention seeking, taking unearned credit

- An emptiness at the core of himself/herself
- Has no meaningful, lasting, and satisfying relationships, and does not connect to others in ways that respect them as separate and worthwhile
- Shallow emotions—only recognizes, feels, and expresses fear and anger, has the words for feeling but not the feeling itself
- Extremely concerned and focused on personal appearance and image

What is also troubling about a relationship with a self-absorbed person is the difficulty in recognizing him/her until some time has passed where you have most likely invested time, effort, and energy in the relationship, and/or have rationalized away your disquiet. This would not be unusual as it is a pattern of such behaviors and attitudes that signal self-absorption, not any one or two of these; some may only emerge over time, others are hidden or masked, and you are not in the habit of analyzing others' behaviors or your reactions. You may sense that something is awry, but cannot identify what that something is. The later chapter on the self-absorbed lover will present a process for identifying the pattern, and some strategies that can guide you to better take care of your self.

Exotic and Different

It's been said that opposites attract and this may be one reason you are attracted to unsuitable lovers who are exotic and different. Because of these differences, you are more inclined to overlook or explain away other signs of unsuitability. For example, the person may be a minority, and minorities in your community find it more difficult to secure employment. This can be a fact, but you will excuse his/her unemployment for this reason instead of looking beyond that to see if his/her behavior indicates continued job searches, education and training pursuits, or efforts to find out where there are jobs available with an intention of going where jobs are. People who are serious about employment usually pursue leads and other such opportunities.

You can be charmed by the difference, excited because he/she is not like others you know and this appeals to you, attractive and eye catching and you like the attention, and/or is a form of rebellion against some aspect of you such as religion. These too are reasons why you would ignore signs of unsuitability and say something about who you are and what you want in life. It could be that it is very important for you to flaunt convention. We'll examine these reasons in the chapter about the exotic and different unsuitable lover.

Care must be taken when considering your reasons for attraction to this type because being different is not a valid reason alone for rejection or unsuitability. There are many reasonable and valid reasons for taking up with someone who differs from you on some very important characteristics such as racial/ethnic group, religion, or country of origin. Just being different does not equate to unsuitability. What are also present are some of the other signs of unsuitability such as no visible means of support. This one alone cuts across all other characteristics, countries, and so on.

SUMMARY

Unsuitability was defined and described, and five types presented. Behaviors and attitudes that are causes for concern in any adult relationship can be especially significant in an intimate relationship where there is considerable intimacy. It is not as easy to walk away, or discard these relationships as it may be for other relationships, or to distance yourself, or to have limited contact. This intimacy is also why it is so hurtful when the relationship does not work, or you find that your trust was misplaced, or you realize that you are not cared for as you care for him/her, or you were betrayed, ripped off, used, and the like. There is a whole host of negative outcomes that can leave you despairing, regretful, angry, shamed, and so on. You are miserable, may berate yourself for not realizing the unsuitability earlier before becoming so involved, and wonder why you were so blind. The material presented so far begins the process for your understanding your self, why you are attracted and overlook signs of unsuitability, and some identifiers of unsuitability. We now turn to a more detailed description for the types, the lures for you and how these develop from an interaction of your personality and past experiences, and suggested strategies to resist the lures.

4

THE HELPER AND THE HURTING AND NEEDY LOVER

A short and unscientific survey of some of my graduate students on the attraction to unsuitable lovers revealed a greater percentage of them selected the item, "need to be rescued, saved or fixed" as the attraction. This lover touches your heart and you want to help him/her to recover from the hurt, and fill their unfilled needs. There is something within you that wants to make it better, or make it go away. You feel fulfilled when you are able to do or say something that helps another person. We'll call you, The Helper.

Exercise 4.1. Am I a Helper Scale

Let's see how much these helper behaviors and attitudes are a part of you. Complete the following scale using the following ratings and assume that none of these are a part of your job, such as a teacher or counselor.

5: Almost always or always; extremely like me
4: Very frequently; very much like me
3: Often; much like me
2: Sometimes; not much like me
1: Never or almost never; not at all like me

1. Friends and family turn to me when they need something and I respond.
2. I listen to others' problems because they need a listener.
3. I like to give advice to help others.
4. I have a soft caring heart.
5. Others look to me to provide them emotional support.
6. I don't do things for others to be admired, but I do feel pleased when others admire me for my helpfulness.
7. I get a charge out of helping others.
8. I look for ways to help others.
9. Giving to others comes natural for me.
10. I work to keep others from making mistakes or doing harmful things.

Scoring: Add your rating to derive a total score.

41–50: You are very much a helper, and probably spend much of your time
    helping others.

31–40: You are a helper and others frequently turn to you for assistance.

21–30: You are willing to help others, but put limits on this.

11–20: You will help others when called on.

0–10: You can and will help, but you don't seek out these opportunities.

Let's take a look at the scale items and explain them.

Turn to You

*Whenever things went wrong, or something was needed, Reggie's friends and
family immediately called him. There was not a day that passed where he did not
get a call from someone wanting something from him, or for him to do something
for them. He grumbled about the constant expectations, but always did the best he
could to not disappoint the person.*

Is this reflective of your experiences? Are you the "go to" person for your
family, friends, and even some acquaintances? How did you manage to get in
this role? While you may be pleased to be helpful to others, do you sometimes
long to be out of this role? Even dedicated helpers can sometimes feel exploited
and that others take advantage of them. These helpers are mindful of the needs
of others, want to be helpful, but can wish that others could be more resourceful
and independent.

If you rated yourself a 4 or 5 on this item, you may have assumed a role
of helper, be responsive and even good at it, and put others' needs ahead of
your own. This is a positive characteristic when you are having to deal with
children or adults who do not have the wherewithal to help themselves, but
not so positive if you are dealing with adults who are functioning and independent, but find it easier to have to take care of them than to do it for themselves.

A Listener

Do you spend a considerable amount of time everyday, or almost everyday,
listening to others' problems, concerns, or tales of woe? Even more important,
do you take these on and make them a part of you, fretting about their
circumstances, and unable to stop worrying about them? Do you assume
some, or all of the emotional distress they feel, and find it difficult to let go of
these feelings? Do you frequently feel that you should do something to fix it
or make it better for the other person?

Having a trusted confidant to listen is a valuable gift, and one to be cherished. It can be encouraging and empowering to have someone like this when
the need is great. However, these occasions should be rare, and not a frequent

occurrence. Just knowing that there is someone who cares and would try to understand can be sustaining enough.

If the description in the first paragraph fits you, then you may find that you are suffering and miserable along with the other person, and your psychological boundaries are such that you are emotionally susceptible. This is one way that the hurting and needy lover captures your interest and is appealing to you. You can reduce some or all of the negative aspects of being a helper by building your boundaries and reducing your susceptibility. This process is discussed in Chapter 9.

Giving Advice

Advice giving can be a part of your trying to be helpful and to fix it for the other person. You've seen the problem, and have a solution. If the person will follow your advice, the problem will be solved—or so the advice giver thinks. There are many complexities that may prevent the advice given from being effective such as the following:

- An inadequate understanding of the situation, so that the advice only addresses a part of what is needed, and that may not be the most important part
- The information provided by the advice-seeker is distorted, or essential pieces are missing, and thus, the advice is inadequate or off target
- The advice receiver's circumstances are such that the advice cannot be followed
- The advice is based on the giver's perspective, experience, and personality which does not fit the receiver
- Advice is a form of telling people what they should or ought to do

You may want to ask yourself why you are prone to be asked for advice, and why you give it. The reasons may surprise you. Examples include feeling useful and helpful, having a sense of power and control, a need to be influential, and wanting to prevent others from doing harmful things. These are not unusual, but you may not have thought of them in connection with yourself. Most of these reasons are positive when they are tempered with an understanding that others are separate and distinct, that advice is a form of telling others what they should or ought to do, acceptance that others are independent and that independence should be respected, and that your needs and experiences are different from the other person's and will probably not fit his/her situation. You need to stay in touch with the very real possibility that you like to give advice to get your needs met, and that the unsuitable lover, on some level, is aware of this and is using it for his/her benefit.

A Soft Caring Heart

Caring about others' welfare on the one hand is a very positive characteristic, but on the other hand, it can leave you vulnerable to taking on others' problems as if they were your own, responding unconsciously to manipulation, having an inability to say no and thus be taken advantage of, and neglecting your needs to be of service to others. You may find that you spend more of your time taking care of others who can take care of themselves than is proper or necessary.

A soft caring heart may also be descriptive of someone who is extremely emotionally susceptible, and easily catches others' feelings. When the caught feelings are of distress for the other person, then the need and desire to be a helper gets triggered, and action is taken to prevent both of you from feeling this distress. The helper can be manipulated into doing things not in his/her best interests, or that are self-destructive. The helper's psychological boundary strength is inadequate to prevent catching and acting on others' sent feelings, and this interacts with the helper's need to take care of others. The helper's strength and positive characteristic is taken advantage of and works to his/her detriment. The challenge is to be able to retain your care and concern for others without losing your self to others' needs and manipulation.

Provide Emotional Support

If your rating for this item was a 4 or 5 then you may be encouraging others' dependence on you to a greater extent than is necessary. We're talking about responsive adults, not children or others who are unable to care for themselves. There are also situations and circumstances where even fully capable adults can appreciate some emotional support, and I hope that you know that your providing emotional support is proper and to be encouraged. These are unusual circumstances for these people, and they are not looking for you to give them long-term emotional support.

Unsuitable lovers can capitalize on your tendency and need to provide emotional support, and make sure that they remain needy to keep you involved and interested. These lovers may not be the only ones in your life that seduce you into taking care of their emotional needs instead of taking care of these themselves. You may want to ask yourself the following questions:

> Am I taking care of others' emotional needs when they could take care of these?
> What do I get out of doing this?

You are getting something or you would not continue to do this and get caught up to the point that you do.

Admired for Your Helpfulness

It's nice to get appreciation and admiration even when these are not sought or expected. You can feel pleased, get a boost to your self-esteem, feel valued by others, and appreciate the recognition. These are all positive and affirming.

The unconscious piece however, may be that you are being helpful to gain admiration and are not aware of your motives. You may not be altruistic where you freely give of yourself without expectations of reciprocity. Instead, you are helpful to get admiration from others. While you are not aware of doing this, others can see what you do not see, and take advantage of it. You become open to their manipulation of your unconscious need, and can find that you are overly committed to taking care of someone who can take care of himself/herself, to do things you do not want to do, and/or to not act in accord with your values and principles. All of this is very complex, and understanding yourself better is the key to prevention of manipulation by others.

Getting a Charge

Helping others can be enriching and can produce many physical and/or emotional benefits for you. People who help people tend to be happier, more content, and healthier. So, if you get a charge out of helping others, you fit right in with many other people who volunteer for community and other services. All of this is really positive and is a part of a meaningful life.

However, if you extend your helpfulness to the point where you are over-committed, neglecting other relationships or duties that are important to you, or other such outcomes, and you are focused more on pursuing the charge that comes with helping others, then you are losing sight of the real purpose and goal for helping. In addition, others can prey on this need you have, and ensure that you always have something you can do for them. They take advantage of your need to help, and also of your need to gain a charge. Your priorities can get out of whack, and you find that you are constantly helping others, don't understand why you cannot refuse them, seek out opportunities to provide assistance, and don't seem to have the time to do many of the things you would like to do. An unsuitable lover can tap into your needs and use these for his/her advantage. You may want to understand your needs better to bring more balance into your life without giving up the positive benefits for helping.

Look for Ways to Help

You may not wait to be asked for your help, you constantly look for ways to be of help. You are alert and aware of what others may need before they realize that they need something. You like anticipating and fulfilling others' needs, and can feel most helpful doing so.

This calls for a high degree of observation on your part, some knowledge of others although your notion of what is needed could be a projection on your part, a desire to prevent others from discomfort or distress so that you don't have to feel the same way, and a strong, but illogical sense of the extent of your responsibility for others' emotional well-being and welfare. You are constantly in a state of anxiety less you miss a clue or signal that others want or need something.

You may not be aware of how tense and anxious you are about anticipating others' needs because you've probably always been that way from an early age where you were expected to read others' minds, anticipate their needs, and provide what was wanted. If this description fits you, either well or very well, then you may want to reflect on how you are extending yourself beyond what is reasonable, give up mind reading and assume that functional adults are capable of getting what they need or at least asking for it, and allow others the space and freedom to be independent from you.

Giving Comes Naturally

Some people find that it requires little or no effort on their part to give to others, and consider that to be a natural part of who they are. Others can find that, while they can give, it does take thought and effort. I suspect that a major part of natural giving is a result of expectations, experiences, and models during the formative years, and may also contain elements of doing for others what you want others to do for you. This, by no means, diminishes the worth of the giving as that is still positive and valuable.

A deplorable outcome for unconsidered giving that seems natural for that person is that some unprincipled people will perceive them as someone to con, take advantage of, prey on, and use them for their personal gains. This outcome is difficult to prevent as you will have to change many ingrained thoughts, attitudes, and behaviors that have defined you as a person for so long, and realize that some people are not as principled as you are, appreciative of your open generosity, but are out to exploit you. You may want to become more discerning about your giving.

Working to Protect Others

If this attitude and behavior is not a part of your job description, such as a nurse or police officer, then you may be reluctant to admit the limits of your responsibility for others, or fostering dependence instead of encouraging independence and autonomy. Yes, I do believe that we should do what we can to protect others, but there are limits, and we need to recognize and accept these.

You may give so much thought and time to this matter that you starve other parts of your life such as your personal development and building important relationships. This can be especially true if you have an unsuitable lover who engages in self-destructive and/or risky behavior. You may give a disproportionate amount of your time, effort, and even money to try to prevent him/her from doing those things. But, he/she is not the first or only person in your life that you assist in this way. You feel overly responsible for others, and act in accord.

YOU AND THE HURTING, NEEDY LOVER

The discussion to this point focused on you as a helper. You probably know or suspect that some of your personality characteristics, attitudes, and past experiences predispose you to becoming attracted to unsuitable lovers who can fall into the hurting needy type. Your scores on the scale at the beginning of the chapter should give you some notion about how important being a helper is for you. It could be beneficial for you to reflect on the items and their explanations, and on your score to gain a better understanding of why you are attracted to this type. This can be a first step in the process of growing and developing so that you make better and more satisfying choices for intimate partners.

You now have the challenge of deciding how to balance your need to be helpful with an attraction so that you do not find yourself in a position where your helpfulness is also a weakness that lets others take advantage of you and exploit you for their concerns. You don't want to relinquish your caring and concerns for others as that can be very positive when used judiciously. Others, at times, do need help, you are willing and able to provide it, and it enriches you. The world could stand to have a few more people like this. However, helping others should not work to your disadvantage, or even heartbreak, such as what happens with a hungry needy unsuitable lover.

All chapters may have some suggestions for needed changes that also fit you and your attraction to this type. But, Chapters 9 and 10 are dedicated to providing material that can help you understand yourself better, and to make needed changes. You are not going to have success at trying to change unsuitable lovers, but you can have success at trying to change yourself, and for the ability to recognize more suitable lovers.

Attraction to the Hurt and Needy Type

Let's turn to a description for why you are attracted to this type. A danger in trying to describe a type is that no description entirely fits everyone. Use the following scale to see if your initial responses to your lovers tend to fall into this type. You may already have determined this, but the scale can identify some specific behaviors and attitudes that can serve as signals in the future that you should be cautious.

Exercise 4.2. What Attracts Me

Directions: Use the following scale to rate the extent to which your lovers tend to exhibit the following behaviors and attitudes.

5: Extremely appealing to me
4: Appealing
3: Appealing sometimes
2: Seldom appealing to me
1: Not at all appealing

1. Closely observes you to try and anticipate your needs
2. Seems very sensitive to your moods, feelings, and the like
3. Constantly does things for you that he/she thinks need doing

  4. Seems to be always around where you are
  5. Details his/her daily, or almost daily, experiences
  6. Listens carefully to everything you say for hidden meanings
  7. Is insistent that you spend most of your time with him/her
  8. Overly affectionate, especially in public
  9. Tells you how much you are essential to his/her life
10. Tells you that you are the only one who cares and understands

Scoring: Add your ratings to obtain a total score

41–50: Appealing
31–40: Strongly appeals to you
21–30: Appealing to you much of the time
11–20: Seldom appealing to you
0–10: Not at all appealing–a turn off

Let's examine your attractions.

Anticipate Your Needs

It can be very pleasing to have your needs anticipated, but it can also become disconcerting to have someone constantly observing and monitoring you for whatever reason. This can get to be very confining and claustrophobic. If this pleases you, it can mean that you and the other person are similar in what you think are expectations of you and in some family of origin experiences. Both of you may have experienced some of the following:

- Children were expected to anticipate parental needs and wishes, and act to take care of these
- Punishment, or abuse or disapproval was the outcome for failure to anticipate
- Children's emotional needs were fulfilled by accident, neglected, or ignored
- Children were valued only for how well they met the parents' needs, and had no intrinsic value
- Children were constantly observing and on edge to try to anticipate what was needed, what was about to happen, and if there was danger to them forthcoming

Sensitive to Moods and Feelings

At first you may be appreciative of someone who shows some sensitivity to your moods and feelings. Everyone likes to feel understood, and their feelings acknowledged. This can be especially refreshing after several experiences with people who were insensitive and even indifferent. The change makes a real difference.

But, sensitivity taken too far can leave the receiver feeling smothered, promotes dependency, and having a need to be cautious about which feelings are expressed. The overly sensitive person can come to feel put upon at always having to respond to your moods, that he/she is inadequate because you have moods and negative feelings that he/she is at fault for not preventing these, and so on. The pleasure about the sensitivity can disintegrate, and the giver can start rage, resentment, and anxiety, all of which is suppressed.

The background for having or needing this supersensitivity is similar to that discussed in the previous section on anticipating. Overly sensitive people have to be hypervigilant because nothing, or little, in their lives has been consistent, predictable, and they had little control over what happened to them. They adopted this supersensitivity as a means of control and survival. It's going to take a lot of effort and guided understanding to reduce or eliminate this hypervigilance, and supersensitivity.

Does Things for You

The important point to note for this item is that this person is doing things for you that he/she decides you need, not what you ask for or even want. They are taking charge. Because the things that they do are probably helpful in some ways, or show some thoughtfulness, or come at a time when you are low in spirits and can use a lift, and when you are inclined to perceive the best motives for that person, you are accepting and even appreciative of what was done. Any disquieting thoughts and feelings you may have are firmly suppressed.

These actions are not without expectations and emotional strings. In return you are expected to be more favorably inclined toward him/her, to be grateful, and to tie you more tightly to him/her. These expectations are seldom if ever explicitly verbalized, but they are there nevertheless. You can find yourself in a state of perpetual debt that can never be fully paid off.

Always Around

You may like the attention and gain some measure of comfort and confidence from having this special person always in your company. Indeed, during the first phase of an intimate relationship, you cannot see or be with him/her enough, and seek more ways to be together. The part of you that craves and yearns for a meaningful relationship and deep connections responds to this behavior. You can become closer, learn more about each other, and shut out the rest of the world.

At some point, this behavior may become too confining and controlling instead of being a pleasure. You cannot do many of the things you were accustomed to doing, some other relationships you have can be negatively affected, you can feel stuck where you are not growing, and/or you can feel manipulated and controlled. You don't have any alone time or time for yourself. Yes, you do want company and companionship, but not all of the time.

It's almost as if the person fears that you will disappear and abandon him/her if he/she is not constantly in your presence. This constant presence today includes being immediately available electronically such as telephone or e-mail. You have to be there and be responsive at any time. You can begin to feel smothered, controlled, and confined.

Details His/Her Experiences

This item may also describe you. Do you find that you feel you need to provide considerable details about almost everything? Is this done to ensure that listeners completely understand? Is this your way of also conveying to others that you want and need details about them in order to feel that you get a complete picture or in order to feel that you know and understand them at a deep level? Does silence bother you, make you feel uneasy, and you counter this with chatter? There are numerous reasons why someone details all, or almost all, of his/her experiences by giving all thoughts, ideas, speculations, feelings, and even fantasies. But, the main reason they do this is for their comfort.

This behavior with an expectation of reciprocity can cause a great deal of difficulty when one person in a relationship is an extrovert and the other person tends to be introverted. The extrovert provides too much information for the introvert, whereas the introvert does not provide enough information for the extrovert. The extrovert can begin to feel like he/she has to pull information out, and does so with many questions that can feel like an attack or suspiciousness to the introvert. The introvert can begin to feel intimidated with information in addition to feeling attached or that the extrovert is untrusting. These personality characteristics can lead to much misunderstanding.

If the initial description fits you, then you may want to experiment with giving fewer details, or even waiting to be asked. If the description fits your unsuitable lover, then you need to understand that he/she has deep needs for reassurance that can never be adequately provided.

Listens for Hidden Meanings

Along with observation to anticipate needs, oversensitivity to moods and feelings, constantly doing things for you, and overattentiveness, this person can be on the alert for hidden meaning in whatever you say. Nothing is taken at face value, and he/she can push extensively for further clarification and revelation of hidden meanings. You may be appreciative at first of how he/she listens to you so intently, and assume that the probes are so that he/she will understand. However, you may realize as time passes that the probes are a part of that person's suspicious nature, and that he/she is convinced that you are hiding something. He/she then becomes very anxious, and probes even more intently.

This behavior too can be an outcome from chaotic and unsettling family of origin experiences where survival was facilitated by being able to discern the real meaning for what was said. Little or nothing could be taken at face value, people were not always truthful but that too was inconsistent, the expectation was that you could read minds and know what the real meaning was, and where there were negative consequences for failure to do so with accuracy. Growing up this way produces a person who is extremely anxious in ambiguous situations that turn out to be almost every situation he/she encounters. You are unlikely to change their expectations and behavior.

Overly Affectionate

Public displays of affection can be spontaneous acts that are brief and enchanting. Overly affectionate displays are continual, smothering, controlling, and uncomfortable for others to observe. These acts are an exhibition of intimacy, done for effect to show off, can be declaration of possessiveness or ownership, and exploits the close connection between the participants.

Although both parties in the relationship are participating in the overly affectionate display, most often it is initiated by one partner, and the other one may have some reservations, but goes along with it so as to please the other person. Or, they may be full participants in wanting to communicate their desire for him/her to the world at large. Whatever the reason, the basic one is not love, respect, or caring.

The hurting needy unsuitable lover who is overly affectionate in public is very likely to be marking his/her territory, searching for reassurance that he/she matters and will not be abandoned, and as a means of control of the other person in the relationship. At first, you may be pleased that he/she is so enamored of you that he/she wants the whole world to see the intimacy of the relationship as you can also have some of that feeling. However, it probably isn't long before you begin to feel some discomfort, and want to cool it in public. If you signal this, either verbally or nonverbally, he/she can become anxious, fearful, and even angry. You have stopped or lessened your fulfillment of the need for reassurance that he/she will not be abandoned, or that he/she is not effective at controlling you, or some other negative perception. No rational explanation is sufficient, and a rift in the relationship can appear.

Essential to His/Her Life

Feeling essential can be very enticing and seductive, especially when this taps into a deep need of yours. Helpers have this deep need to help others with their most important and significant needs, and are drawn to people who seem to need them. The hurting and needy unsuitable lover certainly meets this description, and is one way that the helper gets sucked into these relationships over and over again.

It can be affirming and inspiring to have someone tell you that you are important and needed in their lives as this is certainly a basis for a deep commitment love relationship. You don't want to be in a relationship with someone who is indifferent to you and not committed to the relationship. That's one extreme, and the other is where the other person has you as essential to his/her life. Important and needed achieves a balance between two extremes.

The hurting and needy person does crave someone essential in his/her life because of early experiences, usually in the family of origin, where his/her developing self was inadequately nurtured, needs were not met, there was a lack of empathic responding to the infant and child, and there has been other experiences throughout his/her life that have reinforced these early experiences. This unsuitable lover has many and sufficient reasons for the hurt and neediness. He/she does need something at a very deep level. However, what you will find, and this is why their other relationships did not work out, is that you cannot ever meet their needs sufficiently or adequately soothe the hurts. Their meeting their needs and healing has to come from within them, and any outside agency, such as another person, can only provide support and encouragement for the growth and development. A skillful mental health professional could provide guidance in addition to encouragement and support, but the real work has to be done by that person.

Care and Understanding

Beware if you are told that you are the only one who cares and understands. Yes, you may care more and understand at a deeper level, but if you are the only one, then too much will probably be expected of you. Further, you may want to ask yourself, how an adult who has not been able to relate to others is going to be able to do a complete change and relate to you? There may be good and valid reasons for being alone and isolated, but you may need to be cautious about giving your heart and resources until you better understand how this came to be.

What you are more likely to find out is that this person had and has people who care and understand, just not to the extent he/she wants or needs. They cannot provide enough, and he/she continues to look for what is wanted or needed from outside sources rather than developing his/her core inner self. That development would help nourish, heal, and produce self-efficacy. Since he/she doesn't grow and develop the self, no healing of the hurt or nourishing the needs occurs, and the search goes on to find the person who can provide these. You, as a helper, can be drawn to these deficits, and have a mistaken notion that you can do what others cannot. The outcome is the same with you as it was with others. You can never give enough to satisfy him/her.

Your residual feelings from this perceived failure can be any or all of the following:

- Feeling inadequate and not good enough
- Shame for not being a better helper
- A sense of being exploited, but confusion about how and why
- An erosion of your self-esteem
- Despair and depression at being in this fix
- Guilt for not living up to the unrealistic standard you have of yourself as a helper
- Apprehension and dread and even fear about future relationships
- Hurt, anger, and a sense of rejection

You have a whole host of negative feelings, mostly directed at yourself for not being a better helper.

IDENTIFY THE HURT AND NEEDY LOVER

Following are some behaviors and attitudes that can indicate a hurting and needy person. These alone can be troubling, but when these are present in addition to the clear signs of unsuitability described in Chapter 3, then this hurt and needy person has more baggage that contributes to unsuitability. Rate a part or current lover on the items using the following scale:

5: Always or almost always; extremely like him/her
4: Very often; very much like him/her
3: Frequently; much like him/her
2: Seldom; like him/her on occasion, but not often
1: Never or almost never; not like him/her

Exercise 4.3. The Hurt and Needy Lover

1. Clingy, seems to become anxious when you are away
2. Takes comments personally
3. Sensitive and alert to perceived slights and criticisms
4. Suspicious of others' motives
5. Says he/she is trusting, but finds it difficult to trust others
6. Recalls and tells about almost every hurt experienced in his/her life
7. Whines, carps, and complains
8. Always seems to expect the worst
9. On the lookout for others' taking advantage of him/her
10. Easily hurt by others' comments or responses

Scoring: Add your ratings for a total score

41–50: Definitely a hurt and needy person
31–40: Most characteristics of a hurt and needy person
21–30: Some characteristics of a hurt and needy person
11–20: A few characteristics, but these may not be troubling
0–10: Few or no such characteristics

People who fall into the top two scoring categories are exhibiting a considerable number of behaviors and attitudes that signal hurt and needy. They did not receive something essential to the developing self early in life that continues to exert influences on their lives and on their relationships. Their essential self did not get the nurturing and care needed for good growth and development, and they continue to look for ways to get what was not available at that time. It can be important to note that they are aware of something missing, yearn for it but, at the same time, not be able to know or verbalize what that something is. They seek what they think will fill the void and soothe the hurt, but nothing ever seems satisfying or enough.

This hurt and need is so deep and pervasive that all aspects of their self and lives are affected in negative ways. Some wear their hurt and need visibly and it is easy to see from the very beginning of the relationship. Others put up a facade, and it may take some time before anyone sees beyond that mark. Others can bury these so deeply that it is only over a long period of time that you are able to define it although you were probably aware of it at a nonconscious level.

No matter what you do, you can never provide sufficiently for their needs. You spend considerable time and effort doing the following, but they always seem to demand more.

- Reassurance of their worth
- Empathy
- Affirmation of their existence
- Priority for the needs, and so on
- Sensitivity and caring for their concerns
- Constant attention to them and their interests
- Admiration for who they are and what they do
- Champion their perspective and causes
- Agreement with their position, opinions, and so on
- Changes to your life for their convenience

Scores for the other levels indicate some measure of the same background, demands, and expectations, but these are much less, and may not be as demanding of you and the relationship. However, if they do have some of these behaviors and attitudes along with some of the other signs of unsuitability, they will still expect and demand a relationship with you that does not provide the mutuality of a positive relationship.

Strategies You Can Use with This Type

Following are five strategies that can help you stop seeking relationships with hurt and needy suitable lovers.

- Know and accept your limitations
- Reduce self-expectations
- Be on guard against your fantasies
- Understand how healing occurs
- Attend to your psychological boundaries

Everyone has limitations for their ability to help others, and knowing and accepting your limitations permits you to let others take appropriate responsibility for their own care and development. You don't have to feel that you must do this for them, you can give encouragement and support, but you are not responsible. This way, when you fail to give enough, and you cannot help but fail as no one can ever give enough, you are not crushed by the failure nor do you berate yourself for not being good enough.

Reduce your inflated expectations of yourself as a helper. You cannot always rescue, fix it, or make it better for everyone. This is an unrealistic expectation you have of yourself that can use some self-reflection and examination. You are placing unreasonable demands on yourself, and others, including and especially unsuitable lovers, are taking advantage of your mind set about your self.

Give up the fantasy that you can provide enough of what is wanted, needed, and missing for the other person. Neither of you fully knows or understands what needs to be provided, and hence you are operating on the basis of limited, incomplete, and maybe even distorted information. Your fantasy is that you can know, sense, or intuit what is wanted or needed at all times, and you can feel inadequate when the fantasy fails to materialize. You are trying to do something that no one can do. You may be able to do more than many others, but you can never do enough.

The kind of psychic hurts that we are talking about here occur from birth on, and can be deep and lasting. Some happened during the preverbal period where language had not yet developed, and the information was stored but is not accessible in terms that can be understood after language has developed. This makes it difficult for the person to access and understand many things about his/her own self, and impossible to communicate these to others. Further healing for these kinds of hurts has to take place from within the person, and he/she may facilitate the healing with the guidance and expertise of a mental health professional.

The best strategy can be for you to build and fortify your psychological boundary strength so that you do not catch others' feelings, and thereby you can lessen the possibility that you will unconsciously respond from your helper mode. You will not get caught up in someone else's distress, and set out to fix or take care of it. You'll have time to reflect on the person's behavior and attitudes, check out for other signs of unsuitability, and make better choices for partners for intimate relationships. Strategies for building and fortifying your boundaries are discussed in Chapter 9.

5

THE SAVER AND THE RISK–TAKING AND REBELLIOUS UNSUITABLE LOVER

You may be attracted to the risk-taking and rebellious type of unsuitable lover who provides you with a lot of energy and excitement in your life. You never know what to expect him/her to do, and you are constantly surprised, amazed, and maybe even horrified by some of his/her actions. You see the dangers that could defeat and destroy them, and you feel that they are worth your time and effort to keep them from this dreadful outcome. You can stay in a constant state of edginess and fear. Let's take a look at some of your possible characteristics, behaviors, thoughts, attitudes, and feelings that contribute to your being attracted to this type of person. Read the following list and reflect on the extent to which each item describes you.

- Think that others have more excitement in their lives than you do
- Tend to be cautious and tentative when approaching new situations
- Try to anticipate and prevent problems
- Planful
- Have few interests, hobbies, and the like
- Are thought of by others as being dependable and reliable
- Feel responsible for others' welfare
- Are guided by your role models and heroes
- Get a charge or rush of excitement when associating with people who do exciting things
- Value safety and security

You may find that each item reflects you a little, or a lot. It can be helpful to think of having a collection of these traits, some a little and some a great deal. We'll examine some implications for each item.

OTHERS HAVE MORE EXCITEMENT

There can be times in everyone's life where they feel caught up in routine, or that what they are doing is dull and unexciting, or that they lack something others have that is much more exciting. Nothing seems to fit, you become restless, are dissatisfied with your life, and start looking around for something different. On the one hand, this could be a time for self-reflection and possible growth, but on the other hand, you may cast around looking for something outside yourself to relieve your boredom and dissatisfaction. Almost everyone can experience one or more such periods in his or her live, and it can be a challenge to resolve this.

What can happen for some people, is that they look around them and begin to feel that others have more exciting lives than they do, and have a desire to be more like them. The stories and images in advertisements, film, television, magazines, and newspapers can add to the notion that others have more exciting lives, especially if you are drawn to celebrities, powerful people, sport figures, and other such people in the public's eye. You see and read about their exploits, victories, and successes, and begin to think that you are missing out on something very important. You know that this is only one dimension of their lives, but you ignore the other parts and focus on the excitement.

But, excitement can mean different things for different people. Take a look at what is exciting for you.

Exercise 5.1. Exciting Things

Materials: Several sheets of paper and a pen or pencil for writing.
Procedure: Find a place to complete the exercise where you will not be disturbed or distracted.

1. Sit in silence for a moment, and think about the events that seemed exciting to you in your childhood. Try to recall five to eight of thee events.
2. When you have recalled these, write a list of the events.
3. Beside each event, write all of the feelings you experienced, such as scared, thrilled, happy, and so on.
4. Repeat steps 1–3 for you adolescent years. If you have more than eight events, list as many as possible.
5. Now, repeat steps 1–3 for your adult years.
6. Read your lists of events and feelings, and using another sheet of paper, make a list for the occurring feelings, those that appear two or more times. This list can be suggestive of the feelings you want and are looking for in your life that are excitement for you.
7. Go back to the list of events for each period in your life and classify each event as one of the following:
   a. Physical: roller coaster, sport event, music, dance—use of or effect on the body
   b. Cognitive or mental: problem solving, ideas, or analysis
   c. External affirmation and recognition: receiving an award, selection to a team, receiving a scholarship
   d. Approval from someone you admire: praise, compliments, verbal recognition of you and/or your accomplishments

    e. Internal: a creative process and product, or doing something difficult or
       well
    f. Inspirational: a feeling of connectedness to others and to the universe
  8. Once you have classified each event, make another list of the three most
      frequent classifications such as physical, and inspirational. This list can be
      suggestive of the types of excitement you want and seek for yourself and in
      others.

CAUTIOUS AND TENTATIVE

You tend to "look before you leap," and new situations can make you uneasy. Uncertainty and ambiguity contribute to your cautiousness, and you usually proceed with due care. You do not assume that the new situation can be understood in terms of old ones, that the same behaviors that were appropriate or that worked before will be adequate for the new situation, and may not be sure of your efficacy to handle what may be demanded or expected of you. Hence, you are tentative until you get a better handle on what is happening and what is expected of you. If this descriptor fits you, these characteristics are a part of your basic personality.

There are others who are cautious and tentative because of past experiences that taught them to approach new situations this way. They may have grown up in families where mind reading was expected by one or both parents with unpleasant consequences resulting for not being accurate. It was dangerous to jump too quickly and thus, the person learned to take time to scope out the situation, which has now become an ingrained part of his/her usual mode of being.

Some people who tend to be cautious and tentative can long to be more spontaneous and decisive. They see others act this way without suffering negative consequences, and think that these people are less anxious and don't waste time worrying about what might happen. They just act and move on. Then too, the cautious and tentative person may have been chastised for being slow, a worrywart, indecisive, and so on, and has taken these criticisms to heart. He/she feels that others find him/her dull, plodding, and overly anxious, and yearns for a different persona. These are some reasons why they can be drawn to the risk-taking and rebellious unsuitable lover who seems to have the behaviors, attitudes, and other characteristics that are desired. They also can get some excitement and pleasure from being around the risky behavior, and enjoy taking these chances they would not otherwise take, or doing things that are contrary to their usual behavior.

ANTICIPATE PROBLEMS

Thinking it through to anticipate and prevent problems can be a very helpful characteristic when this does not get in the way of acting. It is certainly desirable to try to prevent as many problems as possible, and/or to develop contingency plans for possible glitches. However, some people can carry this to extremes, take considerable time anticipating problems, worry and obsess over minutia and improbably imaginary problems that they fail to act, and can drain those around them to distraction.

While it can be helpful to do some anticipation of possible problems and take preventative steps, it should not consume the person's thoughts, time, and efforts. Doing so can take a great deal of the pleasure and enjoyment out of the event or situation, leaving the anticipator with feelings of emptiness, deflation, and anxiety that he/she did not think of everything that could possibly present a problem. People who meet this description probably have one or more of the following faulty beliefs:

- Everything must be perfect, and it is their responsibility to insure perfection.
- They are responsible for others' well-being even if the other is a capable adult.
- No one can do things as well as they can.
- They alone are responsible for preventing problems and it is awful if they don't succeed fully.
- It is possible for them to anticipate and prevent all problems.
- Others are, and should be, dependent on them to anticipate and prevent problems.
- It is awful and reprehensible if they should fail to anticipate and prevent all problems.

As you read these, you may want to reflect on the level and extent to which these faulty beliefs drive your actions and influence your life. You may not have all of these, or you may have some to more degree than others, or you may not even be aware of having such faulty beliefs. If you do have some, or all of these, they can be playing a role in your attraction to this type of unsuitable lover.

PLANFUL

This characteristic goes along with the previous one and, when used in moderation, can be extremely helpful to you and to others. After all, these are people whose careers are built around planning, such as event planners and wedding consultants. There are many positive aspects to being planful.

However, there are limits to being planful as one can overly plan, worry, and obsess over details that matter only to that person. People who tend to be overly planful can find that they derive little enjoyment from what was planned, such as a celebration, planning takes more and more of their time; they expect others to be fully cooperative, compliant, and fall in with their plans, and can be very anxious about everything connected to the plan. Spontaneity and joy are missing, they feel this lack, but are locked into the mindset that it is up to them to plan for everything and everyone. They are so concrete, precise, and demanding that others may start to avoid them.

Being overly planful can result from anxiety about one's capabilities, efficacy, and desire for others' approval. They are so afraid that something will go wrong, they will be blamed and/or will feel responsible, and that they will not be liked and get approved. This outcome is to be avoided at all costs, and the only way they know how to ward off this fantasy outcome is to plan, plan, and plan.

Thus, the unplanful person who is impulsive, takes risks, and seems to enjoy him/herself unworried about others' liking and approval, are very attractive. They want to be free of their worry, anxiety, and/or obsession and to be more carefree and unconcerned. But, they cannot seem to break out of their pattern of planfulness, and try to get what they desire to be by association. It is easy to see how and why they are attracted to the risk-taking and rebellious type of unsuitable lover.

FEW INTERESTS

Let's do an exercise to clarify what is meant by few interests—narrow in scope.

Exercise 5.2. Passions and Interests

Materials: Several sheets of paper and a pen or pencil for writing
Procedure: Find a place to work where you will not be disturbed, and that has an appropriate writing surface. I sometimes use a large book for this purpose.

1. Following are eight categories and you are asked to list all activities that fall into each category separately.

   Hobbies
   Pastimes, leisure activities
   Recreation
   Work-related
   Community involvement
   Reading, such as books, magazines, professional literature
   Social involvement, such as clubs
   Other, please specify

2. Begin by writing hobbies at the top of the first page, and then list your hobbies.
3. After you finish that list, write the name of the next category in the middle of the page and list those activities.
4. Repeat step 3 for the remaining categories.
5. Note where your interests are and give each a rating of 1: a little interest, 2: some interest, 3: interesting, 4: very interesting, 5: extremely interesting. Make a note of how many activities are rated as 4 or 5.
6. The items rated 5 are your passions. The items rated 4 are meaningful and important to you. Do you have any passions? For each activity you rated

4 or 5, write beside each how often you engage in that particular activity such as weekly, monthly, or once a year. Then, write the date when you last did that activity.

7. Take note of the categories where you have no listings, and those where you have only one or two. Are there two or more categories where you have no activities listed? Are there one or two categories that have the majority of your activities? This could indicate a very narrow focus.

8. Write a summary statement(s) about your passions and interest.

You don't have to look to others to supply your excitement and interests. Chapters 9 and 10 provide some suggestions on how you can build and develop these for yourself. Doing so could help you reduce your attraction to this type of lover.

DEPENDABLE AND RELIABLE

These are two very positive characteristics unless they tend to put you in a position where others find it easy to take advantage of you because you become guilty and/or ashamed whenever you feel that you fail to live up to these valued traits. You become vulnerable just because you are a nice person with positive behaviors, and others can then try to manipulate you. The challenge then becomes one of preserving your values and principles without allowing others to exploit these for their benefit.

Do the following descriptors fit you?

- You try to keep your promises even at great sacrifice for you, your wellbeing or your relationships.
- You pride yourself on meeting your obligations no matter how distasteful they may be.
- Your guilt can be easily aroused if you fail to do something you promised to do, or that you feel is a responsibility or obligation for you.
- You don't let personal concerns get in the way of meeting your responsibilities, or promises to others.
- Others tend to overly rely on you because you are dependable.
- You feel a sense of satisfaction and accomplishment when others depend on you to take care of them, or admire your dependability and reliability.

If you meet most or all of these descriptors, then you may be open to becoming exploited. It's not that you need to be less dependable and reliable as these are a part of your value system and you like this part of your self. Rather, it may be necessary to better understand why you value these, develop stronger personal limits of responsibility, recognize when you are being manipulated and resist, and develop a stronger sense of understanding of how to help others be more independent.

Responsible for Others' Welfare

Part of being a saver is feeling responsible for others' welfare to an extent that you sacrifice parts of your self in the belief that you must do whatever it takes to see that others are taken care of and come to no harm. When applied to children, the elderly, the sick and infirm, and others who are unable to adequately care for themselves, this belief and attitude is commendable. Indeed, this is a principle or tenant for major religions in the world. But you need to reflect on when does this responsibility end, become burdensome, intrusive, patronizing, actions for personal satisfaction instead of altruism, and/or a rationalization for not acting in accord with your values, principles, and best interests especially when applied to independent adults who are able to care for themselves.

It may be that one of the attractions for you to the risk-taking and rebellious type of unsuitable lovers is your notion that you have a responsibility to save them from harm, and to see to their welfare. You can think that they are misguided, misunderstood, and their positive characteristics are unappreciated, but you also feel that you can keep them from self-destruction. You see and are drawn to what you think are positive characteristics, feel that with just a little encouragement and support they will get on the right track, that you can convince them of how they are harming and destroying themselves and that they need to stop this, and that by going along with their actions you can help them stop, and a whole host of other rationalizations, fantasies, and faulty beliefs about your motives, responsibilities, power, and understanding.

We, as humans, do have some responsibilities to reach out, care for others, and to tend to their welfare. But, they also have some responsibilities to care for themselves, and to seek help when they find that they are unable to do this adequately. Just as you go to a medical doctor when there is a physical problem, so too should you seek out a knowledgeable professional for other kinds of problems that are beyond the knowledge, scope of understanding, and level of expertise for family, friends, lovers and the like. Bluntly said, you have limited responsibility for the welfare of your unsuitable lovers, and you will be better off if you can recognize and accept this limitation.

Value Safety and Security

If you see yourself in some or most of the previous descriptors, you are likely to be the kind of person who values safety and security, although a part of you can long for the excitement and energy that come with risk-taking and rebellion. While safety and security is comforting, you wonder if you are missing something important in life that those who are more adventuresome seem to have so, you are drawn to your opposites. There may even be a part of you that wants to sample what it feels like not to have to be concerned about safety, and to just "let it all hang out."

You may be thinking as you read this that you may fit those descriptors some, but that doesn't mean that you value safety and security, and you may be somewhat correct. So, let's examine a few more descriptors to see how these fit you. Rate yourself on the items using the following scale:

5: I always, almost always, perceive of myself this way, or feel this is descriptive of me

4: I very often perceive myself, or feel this way

3: I often perceive myself, or feel this way

2: I sometimes perceive myself, or feel this way

1: I never, or almost never perceive myself, or feel this way

Exercise 5.3. Safe and Secure

1. Conservative in dress, opinion, and or living style
2. Contained (emotional expression, behavior, etc.)
3. Dull
4. Uninteresting
5. Too "nice"
6. Washed out personality
7. Uptight
8. Overly concerned about others' perceptions of you
9. Unappealing (not sexy, charming, sought after)
10. Conventional (thought, ideas, behavior)

Scoring: Add your ratings to derive a total score

41–50: You very much perceive yourself as unexciting, uninteresting to others, playing it safe, and so on. You tend to be wary of taking risks, and act in accord with society's and parental expectations and use these as the basis for what to be and do.

31–40: You perceive yourself as having some aspects of your behavior and attitudes that seem unexciting and uninteresting, but these are other aspects you feel are more exciting and interesting. You will take calculated risks, ask questions about expectations of you and then decide if you will comply, and don't think of yourself as rebellious. You are more comfortable with society's and/or parental expectations, and may even see some value for these.

21–30: You don't want to term any part of you as unexciting or uninteresting, but you may suspect that some of this exists. You may do and say things to try and prove to yourself that you will take risks, and that you don't always act in accord with society's and/or parental expectations of you.

10–20: You think you have reasons to perceive yourself as exciting and interesting, but you are not entirely convinced of this and have a few doubts at times. You do take some risks in some areas after careful consideration of the consequences, and the same holds for society's and/or parental expectations.

0–9: You perceive yourself as exciting and interesting, take risks, some without due consideration of possible consequences; and do not overly concern yourself with the expectations of society and/or parents.

If your score was 25, you probably find that you are attracted to people you feel are more interesting, exciting, risk-taking, and rebellious. You long to break away and have what you think others get, such as attention and admiration. You tend to minimize your positive attributes, and may fail to see that these others are not happily satisfied, or productive; and that they are attracted to many of your characteristics that you don't value. You may want to reflect on how you can be interesting and exciting to yourself, and build on this rather than looking outside yourself for these.

MODELS AND HEROES AS GUIDES

Part of your faulty thinking that you can or should save someone may be due to the very positive role models and guides you had or have that had significant and important effects on your growth and development. You see and appreciate what these people did for you, and want to give this to others who seem to not have these advantages.

Take a moment and think back over the course of your life, and the people that had the most significant impact on you at different times. These people could have been real or fictional, their impact could have been direct or indirect, the timing of what they gave you was on target or was continual, you tried to live up to what they stood for or expected of you or to behave as they did, and so on. There are numerous ways to have role models and guides. These were some of the influences that structured your thoughts, behaviors, ideas, and feelings about who you are, and how you were to behave and relate to others. They were positive influences.

You may also have seen what happened to peers and others who did not seem to have positive role models or guides, and come to a conclusion that you were supposed to make up for this lack. There even may have been people in your life who maintained that doing so was your duty and responsibility. All of this combined to produce the faulty assumption that you should be a saver, and lead you to relationships with risk-taking and rebellious unsuitable lovers. You are fulfilling what you were taught was your duty and responsibility.

There is much that is positive about the idea of duty and responsibility to reach out and help those who are not as fortunate as we are, and I don't want you to lose sight of this. What is not as positive and may even be destructive for you are the following thoughts, ideas, and feelings.

- I have the power to save someone whether or not he/she wants saving.
- I know what another person needs better than he/she does.
- If only the person could be touched by me, he/she would not do those destructive things.
- Love is so strong that he/she will want to change to please me.
- I have to make the difference for this person or I will have failed my duty and responsibility.

The bottom line is that you can be misled when you believe or think that what worked for you will work for someone else. They are different, and what they need to get on the right track may be not only different from what you received, but may be so basic that neither of you realizes what that something is.

ASSOCIATING WITH EXCITING PEOPLE

By now you may have some understanding of why you are attracted to the risk-taking and rebellious unsuitable lover, and most of these reasons lie within you. There is one final characteristic that merits some discussion, and that is the charge or rush that you get from associating with exciting people. You feel and may think that you are more exciting as a reflection of the other person's exciting persona. This is not an unusual perception, belief, or action as is evidenced by what is seen for the rich, the powerful, celebrities, sports figures, some criminals, performers, musicians, and many others who are deemed exciting.

A lift, infusion of energy, pleasure and satisfaction, and some or a lot of sexual interest are certainly part of what you get from being around this type of unsuitable lover. You probably also get some jealous feelings when his/her attention strays, and maybe even some hurt and anger at some indifference to your actions. But, you can put those aside, or minimize them because you really value the charge you get from the association. You can get to the point where you want to have this feeling all of the time, and think that he/she is the only one that can provide it.

If this description fits you to a large extent, then you may want to think about developing your inner self and resources to be able to supply yourself with some of the feelings you are looking for and receiving from this exciting person. Complete the following exercise to start your thinking and developing.

Exercise 5.4. I Can Be Exciting

Materials: A sheet of paper, one or two $3'' \times 5''$ index cards, and a pen or pencil for writing
Procedure: Find a place to think and write where you will not be disturbed.

1. Write the answers to the following questions on the sheet of paper.
   - When you think about yourself, what about you is pleasing? (Examples: patience, organizational skills, kindness, and so on.)
   - Do you have thoughts and ideas that give you a lift, or are exciting to you? (Examples: solving a problem, making a decision, formulating plans.)
   - How do you express your feelings other than by talking to another person? (Examples: writing poetry, pulling weeds, drawing, dancing, and so on.)

- Can you identify something within you that is inspiring to you? (Examples: determination, perseverance, compassion, a fighting spirit, and the like.)
- What do you think, feel, and imagine that provides a feeling of satisfaction?

2. Write the following on separate lines on the 3″ × 5″ card.

Pleasing
Exciting
Express feelings
Satisfying

3. Beside each of the words on the card, write a list or summary of your responses to the questions in step 1. Use more cards if necessary.
4. Note any omissions as these can be aspects of self to be developed. Read what you wrote, and think of ways that you can enhance these even more.

RISK-TAKING AND REBELLIOUS UNSUITABLE LOVERS

Try to be objective about the person you are considering as risk-taking and rebellious, and rate the extent to which he/she displays the following behaviors and attitudes.

5: Extremely like him/her; always or almost always
4: Very much like him/her; frequently or usually
3: Much like him/her; sometimes
2: Somewhat like him/her; seldom
1: Not at all like him/her; never or almost never

Exercise 5.5. Risk-Taking and Rebellious

1. Impulsive, acts on a whim
2. Says and does provocative things
3. Uncomfortable with calm, silence, downtime
4. Craves excitement
5. Takes unnecessary physical risks
6. Immediately reacts negatively when he/she thinks someone is telling him/her what to do, or what he/she cannot do
7. Scornful, contemptuous, or dismissive of others who are not risk-takers
8. Rejects conventional acts, dress, attitudes, and the like
9. Tend to engage in two or more self-destructive acts, such as alcohol or drug abuse
10. Impatient and rejecting of thinking things through, consideration of consequences for actions, reflection about self

Scoring: Add your ratings to derive a total score.

41–50: This person is extremely risk-taking and rebellious

31–40: This person takes risks and is rebellious much of the time

21–30: This person has numerous risk-taking and rebellious behaviors and attitudes

11–20: This person has some behaviors and attitudes that are reflective of risk-taking and

rebellion

0–10: This person would not be characterized as risk-taking and rebellious

Extremely Risk-Taking and Rebellious

There are times when taking risks can be preferable to other possible options, and many of the explorers, adventurers, and creative people from history moved us ahead in knowledge and civilization by taking risks. So, just being a risk-taker is not negative. So too can be rebellion. After all, that's how the United States was started. Further, some conventions and conventional thinking have lost their usefulness, and new ways of thinking and behaving need to emerge. These can be positive risk-taking and rebellion.

However, what is described here is not positive for intimate relationships. This type of unsuitable lover exhibits uncontrolled behavior, is not thoughtful or reflective, and engages in unnecessary potentially harmful behaviors and attitudes that can lead to harming himself/herself and others. The basic qualities for a meaningful, satisfying, and enduring relationship cannot be established, and the excitement and energy can become edginess and nerve wracking. When combined with other indices of unsuitability discussed in Chapter 3, the resulting behaviors and attitudes are alarming.

You may find yourself with this extreme type before you fully realize what you are facing. In part, this is due to your characteristics, longing and yearning, and much of this happens on a nonconscious or unconscious level, below your awareness. If this should happen to you, there are few viable options that will leave you feeling positive about yourself. The best you can hope for is to gain sufficient understanding so that you are more cautious next time, stay alert and aware to reduce effects of your nonconscious and unconscious on your choices and behavior, and to realize the impact of your need to be a saver on your choices of who gets your heart. You will be well advised to give up the fantasy that you can change another person, and to adopt a more realistic perspective to include changing yourself, and allowing others to be independent and to determine their own fate.

Numerous Behaviors

This person may have fewer of the behaviors and attitudes that characterize the extreme, but the ones possessed are still numerous enough to be troublesome, especially to the relationship. They may be less impulsive, hide their reactions better when they feel they are told to do or not do something. Their risk-taking may be potentially less harmful, and so on. However, the final results are similar to the extreme category, and can still be dangerous for them, for you, and definitively dangerous for the relationship.

These people seem to take pleasure from taking unnecessary chances with theirs and others' physical, financial, and emotional well-being. They get a charge out of others' trepidation, fear, caution, and deliberateness because they believe that these characteristics are dull, limiting, and do not apply to them because they are superior. Their restlessness and edginess can be catching, and you also become restless and edgy. This, in turn, can negatively affect you in the following ways:

- Physical Health: sleep, over- or undereating, nutrition, alcohol and/or drug use and abuse, headaches, stomach distress, and so on.
- Relationships: your other relationships can suffer from lack of attention, lessening of trust, increased concern about your behavior, conflict, and so on.
- Inspiration: less connection to others and to the universe, fewer altruistic acts, less awareness of beauty and wonder, and so on.
- Creativity: no time for reflection, imagination becomes stunted, no time to create or to learn something new—this aspect of self is minimized and overlooked.
- Emotional: milder forms of feelings are missed, overlooked or ignored; more negative feelings are experienced; constant edginess and impatience, and so on
- Cognitive Health: mental confusion, obsessive racing thoughts, inability to concentrate or stay focused, scattered thoughts

Some, Or None, Behaviors and Attitudes

If your total ratings for the person fell into one of the two lowest categories, the person has few if any of the risk-taking and rebellious behaviors and attitudes. He/she may exhibit some measures of one or two of these, but infrequently, and these few times are not cause for concern unless they lead to harm for that person, or for others. They may still be unsuitable lovers, but do not fall into this category. You may want to examine the other categories.

PROTECT YOURSELF

It may become easier to avoid becoming involved with the risk-taking and rebellious unsuitable lover after reading this chapter and completing the exercises because you will have begun the process for protecting yourself by starting step 1. The process has the following steps:

1. Understand yourself and what you are seeking when you choose this type of unsuitable lover.
2. Determine what characteristics you have in common, with the potential lover and where you are dissimilar.
3. Think about and reaffirm your values and what you want in a relationship.

4. Increase your awareness of where you need to grow and develop, and search out ways to accomplish this.
5. Take charge of your own energy and excitement instead of counting on outside sources for these.
6. Curb your tendency to be dazzled so that you can think clearly, and not be led astray by others.
7. Start to value your strengths and other positive characteristics.

6

THE BELIEVER, AND THE CHARMING AND MANIPULATIVE UNSUITABLE LOVER

This type of unsuitable lover could also be called the "con," trickster, or exploiter as these terms are very descriptive of the behavior and mindset for them. Their facade is very deceptive, and it can take an enormous amount of time before you can see beyond this mask, because it is so prevalent and appealing to you. They may, or may not, be aware of their facade as they have spent many years perfecting it, they were reinforced for having it by the positive responses of others, and may not like the self they have behind the mask.

But, a more important consideration is to get some ideas of what attracts you to this type of unsuitable lover. Consider the following questions as they apply to you.

- Why do you fall for the charm?
- Why do you take these people at face value for so long, and in face of evidence to the contrary?
- How do they seduce you?
- How do you convey your wants, needs, vulnerabilities, and desires that can be exploited?
- What is preventing you from learning from your previous experiences with charming and manipulative people?
- What are you yearning, longing, and hungry for that you think you don't have?

We'll expand on each of these questions to explore what they may mean for you.

FALL FOR THE CHARM

Synonyms for charm include bewitch, enchant, enthrall, and spellbind, and all these carry an implication of magic that suggests that one is powerless to prevent the attractions and fascination. That can certainly seem to be what happened to you in retrospect. You did not realize what was happening to you, and you could not prevent yourself from becoming captivated.

If you try to describe what was charming, you are most likely to find that words are inadequate. Any descriptors you use do not begin to capture the allure and fascination of the person you perceive as charming. This is part of the magic and mystique; these people defy description.

Neither can you describe what they did or said that attracted you. This is one area where it may be useful to reflect and try to identify what about the person was alluring and attractive. We'll do more with this later in the chapter.

FACE VALUE

Your life and relationship experiences predispose you to trusting or wariness when first meeting someone, and also play important roles in your subsequent responses. You may tend to be childlike and overly trusting even in the face of considerable contrary evidence. This is not childish, but is very much like children who tend to be open and accepting of almost everyone. However, adults have usually learned that it is not wise to be totally open and accepting of others as they present themselves because experience has taught them that most people take time to reveal their true self, and generally present a "public" face. This public face may not be a mask or facade, it is just the polite and civil public face that can be easily put aside so that the real self can be seen.

You may attend to the mask or facade assumed by the charming and manipulative unsuitable lover because you are still in the child like mind-set of accepting others at face value. You don't like the notion that anyone is deliberately deceptive, and/or intends to exploit you for his/her benefit, so you refuse to consider that as a possibility and blindly continue to trust.

SEDUCTION AND HOW TO AVOID IT

Definitions for seduction include the words corrupt, beguile, entice, and to win over. I'm not sure about the corrupt part of all charmers, but it is likely that beguile, entice, and win over are the motives, intent, and guide the behavior of most all charmers. You can be seduced without realizing it because you are open to being enticed, and this openness and susceptibility is what we will address here.

You can be more vulnerable to seduction if you have most or many of the following characteristics.

- Sustained attention to others
- Value interrelatedness
- Can read and are responsive to others' nonverbal communication
- Mirror others' postures, gestures, facial expressions, and voice tones
- Emotionally reactive
- Are in a state where your insecurities seem to be especially acute
- Overconfidence in your ability to manage and control your emotions

Sustained attention means that you tend to be entirely focused on others with whom you are interacting. Your body is oriented toward them, you maintain eye contact, you lean forward toward the person, and you listen intently. These metacommunication cues convey attention, interest, caring, concern, openness, and appreciation for the other person. All of these are very conducive to becoming seduced.

Value interrelatedness can be a very positive characteristic, but if you perceive yourself mainly in terms of interrelatedness, this can lead you to seeking approval to the extent that you compromise your principles, values, morals, and ethics. You become so dependent on needing the positive feedback from others that you will do almost anything to make sure you get this.

Reading and responsiveness to others' nonverbal communication usually happen on the nonconscious or unconscious level, where you are not aware of what you are doing. Therefore, with the seducer, you can unconsciously respond to his/her nonverbal communication of what he/she wants and desires, and all of this takes place without words. This is one way that you can end up seduced, without any realization of how you got there, and certainly did not have any awareness along the way.

Mirroring others' postures, gestures, facial expressions, and voice tone is also mainly conscious, and conveys rapport, openness, shared viewpoints, solidarity, warmth and positive regard, closeness, and mutuality. So much intent is communicated through unconscious mirroring that it is no wonder that considerable seduction can flourish.

Emotional reactivity means that you identify and respond to others' emotions without any intent on your part, and that you can get lost, enmeshed, or overwhelmed when this happens. Children are very open to "catching" and reacting to others' feelings, and so are some adults because they did not sufficiently develop a sense of their self as being separate and distinct from all others. Their self becomes caught and lost, which aids in seduction.

Acute insecurities can happen to emerge at any time, but can be especially troublesome after experiencing a disappointment in a relationship; dissatisfaction with personal status; situation, attributes, and so on; envy and jealousy for someone's success; failing at anything; and feeling lonesome and/or alienated. These are conditions that promote questioning of one's efficacy, adequacy, and competencies, and a lessening of self-confidence and self-esteem, thus producing conditions ripe for becoming seduced.

Overconfidence. Some of you may be reading this and thinking that you don't fit some of these descriptors because you are aware of what you are doing, the unsuitability, but persist anyhow. The results are the same and you are left asking yourself the same questions as those who are unaware do. What most likely happens to you is that you are overconfident in your ability to manage your emotions to sufficiently protect yourself from seduction, think that you can come close and not be sucked in, but fail to realize when you are being manipulated. You may be able to do these sometimes, but you still find that you are all too often seduced, and wake up later. You can find suggested strategies for taming your overconfidence, which is really grandiosity, in Chapters 9 and 10.

OPEN BOOK FOR EXPLOITATION

How does this happen that you convey your wants, needs, vulnerabilities, and desires so clearly that someone can use these to exploit you? Don't you try to hide these? The answer to the last question is yes, you do try to hide them, and are probably somewhat successful with most people. However, the charming and manipulative unsuitable lover can be especially adept at reading others' mostly hidden traits, and there is a part of everyone that he/she doesn't see but that others do see. This combination leaves you more open than you realize.

But, it may be more helpful to list some behaviors and attitudes that signal your hidden traits so that you can monitor these, and/or reduce or eliminate them.

- Allowing others to invade your personal space, e.g., not moving away when you feel others are too close, or accepting unapproved touching
- Tentativeness when smiling and speaking
- Overconcern with pleasing others, maintaining harmony, and so on
- Giving too much information and details about your personal concerns
- Orienting your body to someone, leaning in toward him/her, and maintaining eye contact
- Dressing to attract attention, or to blend into the scenery
- Constant or continual attention to others' welfare and comfort
- A whiney, or soft, or hesitant tone when talking
- Unassertive, acquiesces to others' demands, expectations, and the like
- Making negative comments about oneself

LEARNING FROM PREVIOUS EXPERIENCES

We all like to think that we can learn from our experiences, and do not repeat the same mistakes. However, there can be some mistakes, such as choosing an unsuitable lover, that reoccur in spite of resolve and determination not to repeat this. If we were to examine possible reasons for seeming not to learn from previous experiences, the following are possibilities.

- Not understanding the elements of the situations where these mistakes happened
- Reinforcing agent for the mistakes are not identified
- Lack of self-awareness
- Undeveloped narcissism such as grandiosity, attention seeking, admiration hungry, and wanting to be unique and special
- Unresolved issues and concerns
- Transference and projection

The *elements of the situation* may not be fully understood so that you do not recognize the warning signs in time to protect yourself. You may not even be able to articulate how and when relationships with unsuitable lovers began, precipitating events, your internal states at that time, and what you observed about the person that captured your interest. The answers to these can be as important as understanding how you compound your mistakes, and end up in a distressing relationship. An extensive exercise is in the appendix to guide you with this reflection.

Behavioral theory postulates that behavior is learned, and that one cause for persistent behavior is reinforcement. That means that you learn and continue to behave in certain ways because you received something—either positive such as a reward or negative such as loss of privileges—that reinforced the particular behavior. It is not possible to provide enough information here to enable you to determine what may have reinforced your behavior so that you did not learn from previous experiences to help you not choose unsuitable lovers such as those described here. You may want to consider the following as possible reinforcers for you.

- Basking in the reflected glory of the charming and manipulative unsuitable lover
- Having others admire you for attracting him/her
- Excitement for being close to someone who has a dangerous side
- Feeling more energized and alive
- Seeing a need for a saver
- He/she says things that make you feel special
- Wanting others to perceive you too as exciting

Lack of self-awareness means that you remain blind to some parts of yourself and, although these may be parts of the self that can always remain out of awareness, these are some parts that others can see and use to manipulate you. It is not easy to accept that you contribute to your manipulation by others, but they could not manipulate you without your cooperation. For example, one way that con people and scam artists stay so successful is because their marks (targets for the cons and scams) are greedy, and looking to get something for nothing. People who are not greedy usually don't get taken in and expect riches for nothing. You may want to reflect on how you may lack some self-awareness, get feedback from trustworthy family and friends, and/or work with a competent mental health professional to become more aware of hidden aspects of your self.

Undeveloped narcissism can also contribute to making unwise choices, and continuing to do so in the face of considerable evidence that this works to your disadvantage and causes you distress, but you do not learn and thus make the same mistakes over and over. It is important to note that you are mostly unaware of these undeveloped parts of your self, and the causes for the underdevelopment rest in your early development experiences. This topic is discussed in more detail in Chapters 9 and 10, but here are a few examples that can help with some understanding. Think about yourself when you read these and reflect on how your behavior and attitudes can exhibit some form of each. Examples are given.

- Attention-seeking: Getting attention from being seen with the charming and manipulative unsuitable lover
- Grandiosity: You have the power to know others so well that you need not concern yourself about their trustworthiness
- Lack of empathy: You don't see beyond the facade, and do not really empathize with this person
- Admiration seeking: You respond to manipulation because the person is convincing with his/her insincerity, flatter, and so on, that you crave

Unresolved issues and concerns persist and affect behavior, attitudes, and feelings in direct and indirect ways. Experiences during your formative years in your family of origin have very strong and important connections to your development, and how you came to be as you are as an adult. The next strongest contributors are other past experiences, especially those that have unfinished business such as bitterness over being treated unfairly by someone you thought was a friend. Your unresolved issues, past experiences that carry unfinished business, and your basic personality interact to predispose you to being vulnerable to charming and manipulative unsuitable lovers. Examples for family of origin unresolved issues could include the following:

- Longing and yearning for the love of a parent who was absent, or neglectful, or who played favorites
- Having to take care of a parent's emotional well-being instead of the reverse
- Expected to put others' desires ahead of your needs
- Feeling ignored, devalued, and/or minimized by family members
- Being the target of continual criticism, blame, and the like

Some past experiences that can carry unfinished business include the following:

- Betrayed by a friend
- Rejected by a girl or boyfriend as not being good enough
- Trusting someone with a confidence who then revealed it
- Unfair and/or untrue accusations
- Taken advantage of and/or exploited by someone you trusted

These topics are covered more fully in Chapters 9 and 10.

Transference and projection can occur at any time, with any person, and both are unconscious processes. Transference occurs when you perceive and react to someone as you did to someone from your past, usually from your family of origin. For example, you could unconsciously be attracted to this unsuitable lover because these are aspects about him/her that are similar to a parent and, although you are not consciously aware of these, they still affect and draw you to the unsuitable lover. You may want to try the following exercise.

Exercise 6.1. Possible Transference

Materials: A sheet of paper and a pen or pencil.
Procedure: Find a place to write where you will not be disturbed, and have a hard surface for writing.

1. Divide the sheet into four columns.
2. At the top of the first column, write the name of someone you think may be an unsuitable lover; either current or in the past.
3. Next, in that same column, list the behaviors that you find attractive. Try to make these as specific as possible. For example,
   - Listens intently when I talk
   - Smiles at me when I enter the room
   - Gives me little pats and touches that tell me he/she is attending to me
   - Looks at me in a way that makes me feel cared for
   - Compliments me
   - I am comforted by his/her presence
4. Write the word mother at the top of the second column, the word father at the top of the third, and either write sister or brother at the top of the fourth, or if you had neither a sister nor a brother, leave this column blank.
5. Next, put a check in column two by each behavior you wrote for your unsuitable lover that is also reflective of your mother.
6. Repeat step 5 for the columns labeled father, and sister or brother.
7. Review your checks. You are likely to find that many of the behaviors that attracted you to the lover, are reflected in one of the columns. This is an example of transference.

Projection occurs when you unconsciously project a trait or characteristic you have onto another person and then react and respond to him/her as if he/she had that trait or characteristic. The next exercise can illustrate this.

Exercise 6.2. Possible Projection

Materials: A sheet of paper and a pen or pencil.
Procedure: Find a place to write and a suitable surface for writing.

1. Divide the sheet of paper into two columns. Write your name at the top of the first column, and your current or former unsuitable lover's name at the top of the second column.
2. Under your name, list the traits and characteristics you perceive in yourself that have also been recognized by others. Examples are such as the following:
   - Kind
   - Sweet
   - Affectionate

- Trusting
- Compliant

3. Now, check off in column two all of the characteristics that you think your unsuitable lover has or had. These checked traits and characteristics could be your projections.

LONGING, YEARNING, AND HUNGRY

When asked what you are longing, yearning, and hungry for, you may answer, love. That's probably what many are seeking, but it can be a little more complicated than just looking for love. The charming and manipulative unsuitable lover seems to be able to tap into your deepest desires and needs, convince you that he/she will meet these, and you fall for that promise. You must identify these, seek ways to meet them that do not involve external sources or other people, and learn what you are doing and saying that unintentionally reveals them to others.

To get some idea about these deep desires and needs, complete the scale using the following scale:

5: Extremely satisfied
4: Very satisfied
3: Satisfied
2: Dissatisfied
1: Very dissatisfied

Exercise 6.3. Deep Desires and Needs

1. The respect shown to me by others
2. Acceptance as worthwhile and valued by others
3. Viewed positively and receive positive regard from others
4. Receive unconditional liking/love
5. My accomplishments and successes
6. The amount of control I have over what happens to me
7. The extent to which I can influence events and other people
8. My likeability as demonstrated by others
9. My physical self
10. My intelligence, and other cognitive abilities
11. The extent to which I am creative
12. I am admired
13. My attention needs are met
14. I receive approval
15. My resiliency and ability to cope with adversity

Scoring: Add your ratings to derive a total score.

56–75: Extremely satisfied
46–55: Very satisfied

36–45: Satisfied
26–35: Some dissatisfaction with some aspects of self
16–25: Dissatisfied
6–15: Very dissatisfied
0–5: Extremely dissatisfied

Scores 25 and below signal moderate to considerable dissatisfaction with some parts of self that may be communicated to others, and which provide information about your deepest desires and needs that can be used to manipulate and exploit you.

Meeting Your Own Needs

The value for identifying these is that you can now begin the process for trying to meet your own needs, to explore and reflect to get a better understanding of the root causes for these, and to start monitoring your behavior to better hide them or to communicate your strengths and positive aspects of self more clearly. You can solicit feedback from others on how to convey your positive points, use others as models, and even resolve some of the long standing issues, concerns, and unfinished business. You may want to pay particular attention to instituting, developing, and strengthening the following so as to present a less vulnerable persona.

- Posture that is straight and upright, not slumping, when standing, sitting, and walking
- Moderate eye contact that is neither sustained nor shifty
- Arms by your side, and not folded over your chest
- Restriction of need for reassurance gesture such as fiddling or twirling hair, rubbing a necklace, tightening the knot of your tie, juggling coins in pocket, etc. These gestures also communicate anxiety.
- Reducing anxiety communication such as jiggling a foot, shifting constantly when seated, hesitant speech, and so on.

Avoid the following:

- Eyes down, not meeting others' eyes
- Shy tentative smiles
- Smiling most of the time, especially when it is inappropriate
- Making denigrating or devaluing remarks about self in the hope that others will disagree
- Providing too much personal information too soon in the relationship
- Becoming overly responsive at the first sign of attention, and/or flattery

CHARMING AND MANIPULATIVE

What are some signs that you may be in a relationship with a charming and manipulative unsuitable lover? You were presented some information about yourself that can contribute to becoming attracted, and now we turn to descriptions for some of his/her behaviors and attitudes. These are in addition to some of his/her behaviors and attitudes. These are in addition to some of the general signs for unsuitability.

- Constantly uses flatter and insincere compliments
- Engages in one-upmanship and goes to extraordinary lengths to "win"
- Deliberately lies and misleads
- Cheats whenever possible
- Looks for ways to gain an advantage over others
- Is not dependable or reliable
- Cajoles and persuades others to do what he/she wants them to do
- Says and does things constantly that seem to be admiring and approving of you
- Can tap into your guilt or shame to get you to do things you don't want to do
- Minimizes your doubts, concerns, and problems

Step back for a little while and try to objectively look at a current or former lover's behavior, and assess the extent to which he/she exhibits each of the behaviors in the list, not just how many are exhibited.

Flattery and Insincere Compliments

Many people respond well to flatteries and compliments as these are positive external recognitions and approvals. Not all flatteries and compliments are insincere, but some can be insincere, and the person providing these is using them to deceive. This person wants the receiver to believe something that is not true, and usually this is for a reason that is beneficial to the giver of the flatteries and compliments, and to the detriment of the receiver.

How do you feel when flattered or complimented? What is your response? You probably feel pleased and appreciative of the attention and approval as do most people. You can then begin to think that persons providing these are discerning, have good taste, and recognize your quality and value. You are reinforced for what you did, said, wore, or have, and that person recognized how good or wonderful you are. These can be positive for the receiver when they are sincere, but can be manipulative when they are not sincere.

Engages in One-Upmanship

One-upmanship is the practice of staying ahead of a competitor, whether the competition is real or imaginary. That is, everyone is seen as a possible competitor, and the person acts to gain an advantage so as to win if competition emerges. The person who engages in one-upmanship has to be perceived as better, ahead, of superior ability, as having more, and so on. It doesn't matter what it is, who it is, or the necessity or lack thereof, he/she is always in competition.

One-upmanship is generally easy to recognize, but not always. Do you know someone who does most or all of the following?

- Whatever happens to him/her, it is always worse or better than what happens to others
- He/she is always able to get or negotiate a better deal than others can
- His/her accomplishments took more effort, or took less effort than others had to use
- His/her disappointments are more, deeper, and more hurtful
- Her/his possessions are of better quality, cost more or cost less, and/or are prized more
- Whatever anyone has or does, this person has or does it better

Having some competitiveness can be a motivator, spur to increased efforts, and in this case, is a positive characteristic. However, it is possible for competitiveness to get out of hand, consume the person, never be fully satisfied, and keeps them edgy and calculating so as to stay ahead of everyone. Such a person can get to the point where he/she will use any means to beat what he/she perceives as competition, or even potential competition. Ruthless, relentless, and manipulative can be some characteristics of this person.

You probably are not able to immediately identify an over the top or out of control competitiveness as you have to hear and see the person in action over time to fully understand just how competitive he/she is. But, if the person engages in one-upmanship much or most of the time, then you can hypothesize about the extent of his/her competitiveness. This attitude is extended to everyone, including you, and you can expect to be manipulated so that he/she can "win." This is one way or reason you may find yourself doing things you don't want to do, or are not in your best interest.

Lies and Misleads

What is meant here is that the person deliberately lies and makes misleading statements in order to further personal goals, gain an advantage, feel superior, and to demean others by fooling them. These are deliberate actions that are used for manipulation, power, and control, and are extremely eroding for any relationship.

You may feel as many others do when you realize that you've been lied to, or someone misled you. Common reactions include the following:

- Feeling betrayed, and even rejected
- The liar thinks of you as a fool or patsy
- Anger for not being astute enough to see through the lie
- Minimized as not being worthwhile and valued
- Shame/embarrassment for letting yourself be manipulated by lies
- Desire to make the person regretful for putting you in this position
- Vulnerable and hurt

Your charming and manipulative unsuitable lover is apt to have lies and misleading as basic characteristics, begun at an early age, and are deep and enduring. Obtaining what he/she wants is of first priority, and he/she may not experience guilt or shame for using these or other such tactics in these endeavors. You and others only or mainly exist to serve him/her, and his/her thinking may be that he/she is free to use you in whatever way he/she wants to get what is needed, wanted, or desired. This is one reason why catching him/her in lies, confrontations, and the like does not produce more truthful behavior. These people care only for their concerns, and see others as useful only to the extent they can help with these.

Cheats

Cheating can occur at all levels from low, such as a machine giving you something free, to extreme such as embezzlement and confidence games. You can even find adults who will cheat when playing a game with a child. Winning the game is more important than anything for this person, but they also derive pleasure from using trickery to win and put one over on someone.

Cheating, especially when deliberate, is not conducive to meaningful relationships, and points out the lack of trustworthiness on that person's part. It also carries the following implications:

- A disrespect for the other person in the relationship
- Mockery for the naivety of the trusting person
- Depreciation of the value of the relationship for the cheater
- The potential and possibility for further cheating is substantial
- The cheater's veracity is in doubt for almost everything
- He/she is indifferent and uncaring about the hurt inflicted on you because he/she makes sure you find out about the cheating
- Fidelity is not a word he/she understands

The same description for the unsuitable lover in the previous section also applies here.

Gaining an Advantage

The charming and manipulative unsuitable lover is always on the lookout for ways to gain an advantage over others, and this includes you. He/she may already be convinced of his/her superiority, greater intelligence, and as being more worthy, and is just seeking additional confirmation by searching out your weaknesses, insecurities, ignorance, and lack of understanding. These are of more interest than are your positive characteristics and attributes. If you are open, have soft or spongy psychological boundaries, and are trusting and believing, then you aid in their search by volunteering much of this information.

Behaviors that can signal the desire to gain an advantage include the following:

- Probing you and others for secrets, shameful acts, and guilt
- Encouraging gossip, actively seeking it
- Quick to point a finger of blame
- Critical comments and remarks
- Inappropriate questioning about personal concerns
- Want to be the first to know everything
- Lying, cheating, distorting, and misleading

Chapters 9 and 10 can provide some strategies to use to build your psychological boundary strength so that you are not an unwilling participant when this unsuitable lover wants to gain an advantage of you. You may also want to pay closer attention to the behaviors in the above list that can signal the intent and desire to gain an advantage.

Not Dependable and Reliable

Dependability and reliability are two very positive characteristics, and when both members in an intimate important relationship have these characteristics then the quality of the relationship is enhanced. Trust and confidence are built, and these are important parts for all meaningful relationships. If you ever have had a relationship with someone who is not dependable or reliable, then you understand how relationships will falter because you cannot trust the other person as much as you would like to.

Think of a current or former lover, and rate the extent to which he/she exhibited the following behaviors and attitudes:

- Felt it was important to keep promises, and made every effort to do so
- Apologized when unable to keep a promise
- Arrives on time, or very close to it
- Calls when he/she cannot keep a date, or cannot arrive at the designated time
- Pretty consistent in his/her values, ethical and moral behaviors
- Keeps his/her word
- Truthful and trustworthy
- Honest with his/her self-disclosure

If this person did all or most of these and was consistent in doing them then he/she is dependable and reliable. If the reverse is or was true, then the relationship suffered as a result of your not being able to depend and rely on him/her.

Cajoles and Persuades

The charming and manipulative unsuitable lover usually finds it pretty easy to cajole and persuade others to do what he/she wants done because others are open and susceptible to the charm and manipulation, and their psychological boundary strength is not sufficient to keep that person away from vulnerable points. This type of unsuitable lover seems to have an uncanny knack for his/her own ends and benefit.

To get an idea of some of your vulnerabilities, rate yourself on the items using the following scale:

5: Extremely like me
4: Very much like me
3: Somewhat like me
2: Not like me most of the time
1: Never, or almost never, like me

Exercise 6.4. My Vulnerabilities

  1. Wanting, needing and/or seeking others' approval
  2. Comfortable only when others are pleased
  3. Overly sensitive to others' needs and wants
  4. Feel responsible for others' feelings
  5. Feeling guilty when other adults seem displeased
  6. Feeling guilty when others are disappointed even when I was not responsible
  7. Take on responsibilities that others should assume
  8. Spend a great deal of time and effort on other adults' welfare concerns
  9. Personal guilt and shame are easily triggered
 10. Feel inadequate and powerless much of the time

Scoring: Add your ratings to derive a total score.

41–50: Usually find it easy to be cajoled and persuaded
31–40: Can be cajoled and persuaded much of the time
21–30: Susceptible to being cajoled and persuaded often
10–20: Seldom susceptible to being cajoled and persuaded
0–10: Resistant to being cajoled and persuaded

Review the items for aspects of self that need growth, development, and/or strengthening. Suggestions are discussed in more detail in Chapters 9 and 10.

Admiring and Approval of You

Everyone likes to receive admiration and approval and we are likely to have a positive perception of the giver. What is meant here is not the usual expression of these, it's when these are constant and used to manipulate you. The person may even have some modest amount of sincerity, but mostly he/she is trying to ingratiate himself/herself so that you are more receptive to becoming manipulated. You want to believe, and once you do, you are hooked and reeled in.

You may be open to this because you very much want to believe this about yourself and appreciate the perceptiveness of the external validation source since you weren't sure about this for yourself. Your insecurities, lack of some self-confidence, need for external reassurance, and other such characteristics may have predisposed you to unexamined acceptance of admiration and approval so that you readily respond and buy in to it. These people are telling you what you want to hear.

There can be other reasons for your receptivity including some undeveloped narcissism that leads to admiration-seeking behavior. This admiration seeking can be a need for external reassurance that one does indeed exist and is worthwhile and valued as the internal state is not convinced of this and has many doubts.

This and other aspects of undeveloped narcissism are discussed in the next chapter in much more detail.

You may want to ask yourself the following questions, if you are in, or have been in a relationship with someone who constantly makes admiring and approval comments to and about you.

- Am I conveying that I have numerous insecurities?
- Do I look for admiration and approval constantly, or from almost everyone?
- How do I feel when I don't get admiration and/or approval constantly, or from almost everyone?
- Do I feel vague, minimized, or ignored when admiration or approval is not forthcoming?
- Do I over respond to admiration or approval?
- What part of my self do I relinquish in order to get admiration or approval?
- How do I admire and approve of my self?

Guilt and Shame

Guilt can emerge when we don't live up to our values, expectations, and standards. However, these values, expectations, and standards may have been unconsciously incorporated, acted on, and endure without conscious thought, examination, and decision. You probably have many of these that you incorporated from your family of origin and other childhood experiences such as school and church.

Shame results when you are not being good enough, and that you are fatally flawed. There are milder versions of shame such as embarrassment where you do not feel as intensely but the feeling about your self is still negative.

The charming and manipulative unsuitable lover may easily arouse your guilt and shame by suggesting the following:

- You disappointed him/her
- You did not do something you should have done
- If you make a mistake, it's because you are flawed (dumb, stupid, etc.)
- You ought to do (be) better
- You fail to satisfy him/her
- He/she expects you to be perfect

- You are supposed to do something or be something, neither of which are specified
- You should be able to read his/her mind, know what he/she wants, and give it to him/her

Once your guilt or shame is triggered, you probably rush to atone or to demonstrate that you are not flawed instead of reflecting on the possibility that this was your unsuitable lover's way of manipulating you. This triggering of your guilt and shame is one way that these people get you to do something you don't want to do, and/or things that are not in your best interests. Because guilt and shame are personal and unique for the individual, it is not possible to adequately address these here. Some information is provided in Chapters 9 and 10 that may be helpful but these are issues that may be best addressed with the guidance of a competent mental health professional.

Minimize Your Doubts and Concerns

Does the person you think of when you read this chapter say or do things to minimize your doubts and concerns about what he/she wants you to do? We are not talking about doubts and concerns about yourself and other parts of your life, just about the relationship and this person's expectations and demands for you. You may have other doubts and concerns, but those are other topics. We are focused here on the charming and manipulative unsuitable lover who is expecting and encouraging you to do things that you wonder about, or have reason to believe are wrong for you, smacks of exploitation, or seem to be demonstrations of their power and control.

Let's suppose that you have some disquiet, apprehension, or doubts about something this person is proposing that you do. You try to express this, but he/she does any or all of the following:

- Brushes it off as trivial and inconsequential
- Tells you that he/she knows best
- Characterizes you as illogical, irrational, or overly concerned
- Tells you that if you were adequate, you would do it
- Threatens to leave

Instead of respecting you and taking your concerns seriously, he/she is trying to manipulate you by making light of these, seeking to have you feel inadequate if you don't comply, and arousing your fear of losing the relationship. This state of affairs for the relationship is not likely to improve, nor will he/she at some point begin to take you more seriously and really listen to your doubts and concerns. This person is focused only on what he/she wants, and can be ruthless and relentless in pursuing them.

7

THE MIRROR AND THE SELF–ABSORBED UNSUITABLE LOVER

The chapters discussing the hurting and needy, risk-taking and rebellious, and the charming and manipulative unsuitable lovers first discussed your possible traits and characteristics that predispose you to become attracted to them. After that, some of the type's defining behaviors and attitudes were described, along with how these could be alluring to you because of how you are, and gave some possible strategies and changes that, when implemented, could help resist the attraction and prevent you from becoming involved in an unsuitable relationship. This chapter is different in its presentation.

Your role with the self-absorbed unsuitable lover is to function as a mirror, and you do so because that person also reflects some things about you. Thus, the characteristics and traits that are alluring to you about him/her are also ones that you possess in some form, either more or less than he/she does. You and the other person mirror each other, but neither of you are aware of these similarities, nor are you aware of these characteristics and traits within your self. You may see them in each other's behavior and attitudes, but remain oblivious to them for yourself. Not being able to separate these for you and the unsuitable lover means that the usual format for other chapters could not be used for this chapter. The format here combines the descriptions, but also gives suggestions for more self-awareness and strategies for changes. This is one reason why your role is termed "the mirror."

Lets begin by describing some categories for behaviors and attitudes that are reflective of self-absorption. Keep in mind that the person who exhibits these is unaware of doing so, and that he/she is closed to the notion that these exist for him/her. You, as is everyone else, are blind to this part of your self, and will probably deny that any of this describes you. For the moment, let's just accept that some possibility may exist for you, and focus more on the unsuitable lover you believe to be self-absorbed.

The behaviors and attitudes are categorized as

- Inflated self

- Indifference to others
- Impoverished self

The inflated self is exhibited through grandiosity, an entitlement attitude, has to be unique and special, arrogance, and contempt for others. This sense of self-importance is overblown, unrealistic, and unable to accept any idea of having imperfections, flaws, or weaknesses. There is also a conviction of his/her superiority and of others' inferiority. Nothing dents or deflates the inflated self. It is all about them.

Indifference to others is reflected in behaviors and attitudes that show a lack of empathy, inappropriate humor, exploitation of others, and an inability to recognize and respect others' boundaries. All, or most all, of their energy and focus are on them, with little or no recognition or respect for others as worthwhile individuals.

The impoverished self is the other side of the inflated self, and both exist at the same time. The outer manifestations can rapidly switch from one to the other so that by the time you finish responding to the presenting state, the other one has taken over and your response is then wrong! That can be very frustrating. The behaviors and attitudes that compromise the impoverished self include shallow emotions, admiration hungry, attention seeking, and emptiness at the core of the essential self.

Think of self-absorption as ranging from complete and constant such as expected of the infant and child, to scant and rare such as expected of mature adults. Infants and children have not yet developed any sense of their self as being different and distinct from others, and that their needs and wants should be promptly and properly attended to without any delay.

As the child grows and develops, so should the understanding of their self as separate and distinct from others, as should their ability and acceptance of responsibility to meet their personal needs and wants. When this expected growth, development, and understanding does not occur, the results can be an adult who remains in an earlier stage of self development who has considerable self-absorption, an adult who has many areas that still need developing, or adults who have some to few areas that need developing. You will see as you read further that there are numerous possible variations for both lack of development as well as for developed areas. The important point is that these can be possible self-absorbed behaviors and attitudes for almost everyone, including you, and that it is possible to continue to grow and develop in positive ways if you want to.

Let's move to a fuller explanation of these self-absorbed behaviors and attitudes. Each will be presented with a list of descriptive behaviors that reflect the self-absorption, and as you read these you have three tasks.

1. Think about yourself and how you may be doing these or something similar. The ones you identify as your behavior can then be designated for change.

2. Think about the unsuitable lover and decide if he/she does these or something similar. A few such behaviors may reflect a need for further development, but not necessarily self absorption that is a pattern or a collection of behaviors and attitudes that are troubling to their relationships. However, having many such behaviors and attitudes can signal considerable self-absorption that is troubling for relationships.

3. Back to yourself. Reflect on the feedback and/or criticism you've received about any of the behaviors and attitudes to try and objectively examine these for any validity, especially when the same feedback and/or criticism have been given by more than one person, and/or over a period of time. Doing so can help you see a part of your self that you are blind to, but that others see.

THE INFLATED SELF

We begin with grandiosity, a sense of being omnipotent and omnipresent, that the world exists and things are done only because of you. The infant and child exhibit expected grandiosity where the world is composed only of them and their wants. An adult who has grown and developed has moderated this perception to be more logical and in line with objective reality. But there are many behaviors and attitudes that can be reflective of grandiosity that fall between the two extremes. You, and your unsuitable lover, may have some or many of these, such as the following:

- Think or feel that you can cause or make another person change
- Overextend oneself and take on too many activities, or promises, or financial concerns
- Know what others should or ought to do, and are not shy about telling them so
- Flamboyant in gestures, speech, and/or dress
- Overconfident, cocky
- Fail to understand the limits of personal responsibility, tend to take over in many situations
- Fail to follow rules, policies, guidelines or even laws
- Engage in unethical behavior
- Take unearned credit, and/or credit that belongs to someone else
- Constantly takes more than his/her fair share

You will also see some elements of grandiosity in the descriptions for entitlement, unique and special, arrogance and contempt, and the reverse as these can overlap and intertwine so that it is not easy to separate them. But, they all point to an inflated self that overemphasizes self-importance, and self-esteem.

Entitlement

An entitlement attitude can be very infuriating and frustrating for others. It is an unconscious assumption that you have the right to do whatever you want to do, and others should know that, accept it, and facilitate your accomplishing it. Some common entitlement attitudes include the following:

- Giving orders with expectation that they will be promptly obeyed without question or protest
- Borrow, take and/or use others' possessions without their permission
- Others should insure that you receive preferential treatment
- Others do not have the right to say no, or to refuse you anything
- You are automatically in charge, and others should listen to you
- Others should agree that you deserve more than your fair share
- You should receive rewards without having to do anything
- You can do what you want, where you want, and there should be no questions by others
- You should never have to suffer any penalties for infractions of rules or policies, or for your illegal acts

The behaviors that result from an entitlement attitude are usually very demeaning and devaluing of others without conscious intent. You simply do not perceive them as such and feel that others who question, make comments, or protest are failing to see the rightness for what you said or did. Consider the following for examples of what is meant. Have you been the recipient of any, or have you done any?

- Cut in line, and not wait your turn
- Tell someone how he/she is inadequate without him/her asking for your opinion
- Use a person's possession without first asking for permission
- Entering someone's room, office space, or personal space without explicit permission
- Touching without permission, and this includes children
- Expect someone to do a personal favor for you no matter the cost and effort for him/her
- Expect others to be available for your convenience such as every time you call them
- Expect others should go along with your suggestions, desires, and wishes

These are only a few of the numerous behaviors that signal an entitlement attitude, and they are the sort of things that children do that can be expected at their age. Children don't seem to recognize others' possessions as not available for them, but also consider their possessions as theirs alone.

Children constantly violate others' physical and psychological boundaries, think that their needs and wants should receive priority from everyone, and that others exist only to serve them. When these are carried over into adulthood, they are so ingrained that the person who has them is very much unaware of this.

Unique and Special

Everyone is unique and special, but not everyone expects, demands, or requires that others must always recognize their personal unique and special qualities. Some self-absorbed people, on the other hand, do expect that everyone recognizes and appreciates this about them, and can be very upset at anyone who fails at this. These people can go out of their way, over the top, and to excess in this endeavor. Following are some thoughts and behaviors reflective of self-absorption for this characteristic. While thoughts may have to be inferred, it would not be unusual for this person to speak of these, thus reducing the need for inference. Do any of these fit you?

- Feel that you don't have to meet the same standards as do others, such as for promotion and raises
- Others should recognize how special you are and praise you, even for minor things
- Describe to others how you "stand out from the crowd"
- Like and approve only of people who think you are as wonderful as you think you are
- Constantly and loudly acclaim your accomplishments
- When your children, relatives or even friends accomplish something noteworthy, you make sure that everyone understands how you played the major role for this
- Status seeking, such as associating with people you think have higher status than you do
- Overextended financially in the effort to appear of higher status or to "show off"
- Feel that you should not have to "pay dues," work and wait for recognition

It's not enough to be unique and special, others must defer to this, and should also be aware of how they are lacking.

Arrogance and Contempt

Overpresumptuous, obtrusive, and disdainful are three adjectives to describe arrogant behavior—a display that conveys an overly important perception of oneself. Common terms for arrogance include haughty, high and mighty, hoity-toity, and supercilious. As you read these, you may be shaking your head no because you couldn't possibly exhibit any behavior reflective of arrogance.

But what about contempt? Adjectives for contempt include overbearing, disdainful, scornful, and despising. Contempt, in its many forms, is disrespect for others. You may also think that none of these fit you. And you may be correct for both.

On the off chance that you may be blind to some unconscious behaviors and attitudes that signal arrogance and contempt, let's take a look at some of these. Further, you may not exhibit these, but you may have observed them for your unsuitable lover.

- Openly disparaging of others who differ in race, religion, socioeconomic status, intelligence, and so on
- Categorization of others as acceptable or unacceptable because of an observable difference
- Minimizing or ignoring others' accomplishments while, at the same time, inflating his/her accomplishments
- Become angry when someone does not acknowledge his/her importance
- Expect or demand to be preferentially seated in a crowded restaurant
- Take for granted that he/she will be at the helm of all organizations such as social clubs
- Has an air of looking down his/her nose, and/or nose in the air—conveys haughtiness
- Pompous in talk, posture, and relating to others
- Expectation that he/she deserves rewards, promotion, and other such recognitions and not have to work as hard as others for these.

As you can see from this brief discussion, a description for arrogance and contempt is difficult to put into words that adequately convey how others perceive this person. You will have to be a very open person to objectively review your thoughts and behavior for these traits.

INDIFFERENCE TO OTHERS

The indifference to others that self-absorbed people display is one of the main reasons why you cannot get through to them and have them realize the negative and troubling impact of their behaviors and attitudes on others and on their relationships. They are indifferent, and no amount of telling, selling, demanding, or confronting will cause them to begin caring, and to change.

Lack of Empathy

By far the most troubling indifferent behavior is the lack of empathy. The capacity to be empathic is a characteristic of healthy adult narcissism, and is a critical and crucial component for meaningful enduring intimate relationships. Its importance cannot be over emphasized. Being empathic includes the following:

- A recognition and appreciation for others as worthwhile unique individuals
- Respect for the independence and distinctiveness of others
- An awareness of self as distinctly different from others in the world
- The ability to stay centered and grounded and not become enmeshed or overwhelmed with others feelings
- The capacity to open oneself to enter the world of the other person and sense what he/she is feeling, but not get lost or mired in them

- Maintaining a respectful and nonjudgmental attitude
- The willingness to stop talking and listen to the other person

How can you recognize when you or someone else is not being empathic? The following thoughts and behaviors can signal empathic failure.

- Become bored when someone is talking
- Thinking about other topics than the current one the speaker is communicating
- Getting caught up in the story and its details
- Asking questions to try and show interest
- Focus on something or someone other than the speaker
- Failing to respond at all, or not directly responding
- Ignoring emotionally laden remarks
- Changing the topic
- Saying or thinking what the speaker should or ought to do
- Inferring the speakers' motives
- Telling the speaker what you would do—advice giving
- Wanting to just get away

What are some feelings you experience when your unsuitable lover fails to empathize with you? You probably feel the following:

- Devalued, as if you were not meaningful or important enough for his/her attention
- Not cared for
- Inadequate and insecure
- A lessening of self-confidence
- Anger for being discounted
- Unheard and unloved
- Minimized as a person
- Dumb and stupid for thinking that he/she cared enough, or that your concerns should receive attention

These are all uncomfortable feelings that are eroding to one's self-esteem. When you don't receive empathy from the important people in your life, you can begin to feel worthless, helpless, and hopeless. Some people get away from these negative feelings about self by repressing and denying them, substance abuse or other self-destructive acts, and/or by moving on to a new relationship that holds more promise for fulfilling this need. The latter is usually futile, but that doesn't stop them from leaping from relationship to relationship. You may want to take a look at yourself to see if any of this fits you, and especially to ask yourself if you are failing to be empathic in many of your relationships and interactions. Building the capacity to be empathic is discussed in Chapter 9.

Inappropriate Humor

What kinds of things promote humor and laughter for you? Could your humor be characterized as inappropriate? Humor can be a source of fun, and it lifts spirits, and ward off the blues or depression. The act of laughing seems to promote the release of tension, and to reduce stress. These are all positive outcomes for humor and laughter.

An appropriate sense of humor is characteristic of healthy adult narcissism, and is one to be cultivated. So, how is appropriate humor defined, and how is inappropriate humor identified? Appropriate humor pokes fun at folly, absurdities, irrational and illogical acts, and the like. Inappropriate humor pokes fun at who and what people are, that is, characteristics about them over which they have no control, nor can these be changed. Poking fun at these is the attempt to show how these people are inferior and you are superior. Targets for inappropriate humor include the following:

- People with disabilities
- People who are different such as race, socioeconomic status, and place of national origin
- Mistakes people make because of difference or ignorance, and these are thought to demonstrate their inferiority
- Fooling someone to demonstrate superiority
- Clumsiness and uncoordination that is perceived as a demonstration of inferiority
- Mockery of someone's beliefs, values, and the like

Take a look at the ads, TV shows and movies, comics you like, and identify what you seem to find humorous in these. If you tend to laugh at any of them, then your humor is not as appropriate as it could be. For example, do you laugh at blonde jokes that assume blondes are dumb? Or, are there racial, gender, and/or age-related comments, stories, or jokes that produce your laughter? All of these point to inappropriate humor. Your unsuitable lover has an inappropriate sense of humor and if one attraction for you is that you laugh at the same things, then you too have this.

Exploitation of Others

Taking advantage of others for personal benefit or gain is the essence of exploitation. The other person is manipulated, bullied, forced, or persuaded many times without being aware of what is happening to him/her. When you take advantage, you misuse your power, relationship, position or role to meet your needs and desires without any regard for the other person. They exist to serve you, and you think you have a right to use your advantage.

Just as with anything else, there are degrees of exploitation, and you may not fit the description for the extreme. However, you may find that you do display some level of exploitation such as the following:

- Ask or expect favors without reciprocity
- Give orders and expect prompt compliance
- Persuade someone to do something he/she doesn't want to do
- Make unreasonable or unrealistic demands

- Expect others to use their resources, such as money, to meet your needs and wishes
- Do and say things that produce fear for the other person that you will abandon the relationship
- Suggest that if the other person loved and valued you, he/she would comply with your wishes
- Compliment someone, or flatter him/her as a means to get him/her to do what you want

Exploiting others even mildly shows a lack of respect for the integrity and value for them as worthwhile, separate, and distinct individuals. Instead, you feel that they are under your control and are supposed to do what you want. These thoughts and feelings may not be blatant or even conscious on your part, but your actions reveal the unconscious assumptions. Think about how you may be doing any of the following, and how you could reduce or eliminate these.

- Take advantage of someone's ignorance
- Tell, order, or demand that someone do something for you that you could do for yourself. This includes children.
- Know that someone is willing to please and we use this to ask favors
- Threaten the loss of the relationship for noncompliance with your wishes or demands
- Try and get others to give you their resources

You may also want to take some time to reflect on how your self-absorbed unsuitable lover exploits you, and how you feel about this behavior now that you are more aware of it. He/she may engage in exploitation at a higher level than you do, but you are still mirroring that characteristic and behavior.

Boundary Violations

The indifference to others' attitudes is revealed by boundary violations with both physical and psychological boundaries subject to violation. These actions reveal that the violation has an incomplete understanding of where he/she ends, and where others begin so that he/she intrudes too far over into others' physical and psychological space. Let's try to describe some of these violations. We'll do physical violations.

- Sitting or standing too close so that the other person becomes uncomfortable
- Touching without permission, such as patting a pregnant woman's stomach, hugs, and ruffling a child's hair
- Sustained eye contact or staring where the other person becomes uncomfortable
- Entering a person's personal space, such as their bedroom or office, without first asking for permission or knocking
- Moving someone's possessions so that you can have the space
- Borrowing or using others' possessions without their permission
- Rearranging others' possessions or space to suit you

Psychological boundary violations can be a little more difficult to describe. However, these can be very upsetting or wounding for the receiver.

- Asking personal intrusive questions
- Put downs, demeaning or devaluing comments
- Pushing for agreement and/or compliance
- Demands that others comply with your orders
- Inappropriate humor, sarcasm, and the like
- Comments that suggest the others' inadequacies
- Revealing others' shameful acts
- Negative comments about a person's personal appearance such as weight, hair, and clothes
- Telling others what they should or ought to do

These behaviors and actions tromp all over the other person's defenses and boundaries, and intrude uninhibited into their psychological space where they are most vulnerable. Others may not be able to prevent these, and this can be especially true for the persons in intimate relationships with each other. Intimate relationships usually involve opening of the self to the other which allows for more ease to engage in psychological boundary violations.

You may want to reflect on the violations that you engage in and use these as a basis for planned change. More suggestions are provided in Chapters 9 and 10.

The Impoverished Self

Although the impoverished self can be a flip side of grandiosity, there are also some behaviors and attitudes that not only suggest this, but can also be the prominent characteristic of a destructive narcissistic pattern where the grandiosity seldom or ever surfaces to be visible to others. Think of the impoverished self as the part of the person who did not get some important needs met early in life as is generally expected. For example, babies and children seem to thrive when they get sufficient attention, admiration, respect and understanding of their feelings and are allowed to become independent and separate. They develop self-confidence, adequate but not inflated self-esteem, autonomy, and awareness and appreciation for others in the world as separate from them, and are centered and grounded at the core of their self. They meet the criteria and definition for healthy adult narcissism that includes empathy, a sense of responsibility, wisdom, creativity, zest for life, meaningful and satisfying relationships, creativity, and inspiration. But, let's examine some indices of the impoverished self.

Attention Seeking

To get an idea of why someone engages in attention-seeking behavior, reflect on your feelings for the following situations.

- You go to a party, and no one talks to you
- You are ignored at a family gathering
- You never get to finish what you want to say as others interrupt you
- Your thoughts, ideas, and feelings are minimized
- No one asks you for your opinion or suggestion
- You say you do or don't want to do something and it's as if you had not spoken
- You get attention when you are loud, or acting outrageously

Now, think of how children and adolescents behave to garner attention. They move around a lot, talk and laugh loudly, intrude into conversations, dress and behave outrageously, fight, and do other such acts that get them the attention. While you may consider the negative aspects of this kind of attention to be negative, they will take any kind they can get, so too, do some adults act and feel. They crave attention and can go to extraordinary means to get it, not all of which are positive or constructive.

Review the following behaviors to identify which, if any, are descriptive of your and/or your unsuitable lover's usual behavior.

- Sulking
- Stir up discord, dissention, or conflict, especially among others
- Become more needy, clingy and/or miserable so that someone will attend to you
- Create crisis where you need to be rescued
- Loudly talking
- Interrupt speakers
- Make "grand" entrances and/or exits
- Cry a lot
- Tattle, gossip, and the like

It would not be unusual to exhibit most of these behaviors from time to time, but when these are constant and a part of a person's usual behavior, then it is most likely that there is a strong and unconscious need for attention. What can be helpful as a first step toward understanding your need for attention is to identify the feelings you experience just before you act to get attention. You may be feeling ignored or minimized, that others are not aware of your existence, that you will disappear if you are not actively noticed by others, or feeling isolated and alienated as possible examples. The strategies presented in Chapters 9 and 10 can be additional steps to learn to take care of your attention needs, and to reduce attention-seeking behavior. If your unsuitable lover has strong attention-seeking needs and exhibits many and constant attention-seeking behaviors, you may need to accept that you will never be able to give enough to fulfill these.

Admiration Hungry

The constant and continual search for external validation of one's worth and value can lead to admiration-hungry behaviors. The person craves reassurance that he/she is wanted, cherished, and superior, and is never able to adequately fulfill this deep and enduring need. Approving and admiring by oneself is inadequate, and others' recognition is a necessity to feel adequate and/or superior. This is the person who demands that others perceive him/her as wonderful as he/she does because that external validation allows and supports his/her internal state of being wonderful. Without the external validation, the internal state will cease to exist, and the person will no longer think he/she is wonderful.

Need for external validation can be one reason some people like your unsuitable lover constantly move from one relationship to another, and are likely to have many failed relationships. These people did not get enough of the necessary admiration, or felt that it was diminishing. When this happens, their inner perception of their wonderfulness starts to erode and they must move to find the necessary external validation before all of the inner perception disappears. This support is vital to their existence. What are some admiration hungry behaviors?

- Boasting and bragging
- Taking unearned credit for others' work
- Basking in the reflected glory of others' accomplishments, and assuring every-one that they "caused" the accomplishment
- Whatever they have or do, they present it as better, bigger, and of more worth than others
- Say and do things to garner compliments and praise
- Compliments and praise for others somehow gets turned around to them
- Inflate the importance of their activities, work, and the like
- Engage in considerable self-praise, self-aggrandizement
- Do and say things that are intended to show how wonderful they are

Wanting to be admired is not unusual, and when others make admiring comments that can be very pleasing. External validation and approval is not to be lightly dismissed as it is reinforcing for the self. What is not constructive is to be constantly seeking, demanding, and acting to get this as a goal, instead of building the self to be self-admiring, other inner resources, or accomplishing something that bring sincere and true admiration.

Shallow Emotions

Do you have a wide range of emotions that you experience and express, or do you have just a few? Some people grew up in families where emotional expression was not only discouraged; there could also be unpleasant penalties for doing so. People from these families learned early in life that it was safer and more acceptable to stuff their feelings. Thus, they are left as adults with subdued or even a lack of emotional expression. It still may not seem safe to them to allow themselves to experience and express their feelings. There are also some people, many of whom fit the previous description, who have the words for emotions but not the feelings themselves. They know on a cognitive level what others mean by the words, but do not ever experience those feelings themselves, except for possibly fear and anger.

As the self grows and develops in healthy and expected ways, a variety of emotions are experienced, and we learn to label these so as to communicate our internal experiencing accurately to others. When the self does not develop, or is delayed in developing, then the person does not learn to experience and express a wide variety of emotions. A rich emotional life is not available or accessible to them.

Reflect on your day to this point, or to the previous day and identify the emotions you experienced, and those you openly and directly expressed. It may help to write two lists and compare them. Were there many or few emotions experienced? Were few, many, or none openly and directly expressed? Why, or why not? The truthful answers to these can provide you with more understanding of your self.

Now, turn to reflection about your unsuitable lover. Reflect on your last interaction with him/her and identify how many different emotions he/she openly and directly expressed. Were there many, just a few, or just one or two? Think about his/her emotional expression over the course of the relationship and identify the various emotions he/she expressed. Answer the same questions for him/her as you did for yourself.

Suppose that your life circumstances did not foster or encourage your emotional development, and you don't have a wide range and variety of emotions you are aware of experiencing or openly and directly express. You don't have to remain in this state and can learn to increase your emotional capacity. Some exercises are presented in Chapters 9 and 10 to get you started. Here is a quick exercise to get you started thinking about expanding your feeling vocabulary.

Exercise 7.1. Feeling Vocabulary Enhancement

Materials: A sheet of paper, and a pen or pencil for writing.
Procedure:

1. Write these words at the top of the page so that four columns are created.

       Happy   Sad   Anger   Love

2. Take each word one at a time, and write all associations you can think of for that word. Don't edit or evaluate your associations, you can add to the list as other associations emerge.
3. Next, make an association for each of the words for each of the following:

       A color   A type of food
       A song or type of music   An activity
       A kind of weather   A sensation in your body

4. Finally, read your list associations and write summary statements for each emotion.

Emptiness

The emptiness referred to here is at the core of the self. There is a void where nothing exists, and that is very frightening. It's hard to put into words what emptiness within is like and my description probably falls short of what experiencing that is like for the person. Closely related to the emptiness of the self-absorbed person are depression, loss, and isolation and alienation. But these are temporary conditions that one can take action to do something about to relieve. Contained in these states are many feelings, usually negative ones. There can be anger, guilt, shame, remorse, and fear. The same is not true for feeling empty. There are no emotions there to access, and the person experiencing emptiness does not have resources to begin to do something about changing the emptiness.

Since emptiness is very frightening, people will go to extremes to keep from having to experience it. They fill their time with many activities, many of which have little or no meaning and/or are self-destructive. They abuse substances, such as alcohol and/or drugs, and may search out and participate in very risky undertakings just to ward off the fear that surrounds any idea of the emptiness within.

You may want to explore the following questions for yourself, and for your unsuitable lover.

- What meaning and purpose are these for the time and effort spent on most activities in your life? Why do you do what you do?
- Can/do you experience joy? Reflect on why or why not.
- Do you take steps to not be alone? Do you always have to have something or someone active around you? Does silence seem threatening and produce anxiety for you?
- Think of your life, and note what and how many satisfying, meaningful, and enduring relationships you've been able to form and maintain. Are there any such relationships?
- Do you have any deep and meaningful relationships?
- Do you feel loved, cared for, cherished, and valued by anyone?

These are difficult questions to explore for anyone, and may be especially so for those who fear they are empty. If you find that you become anxious when thinking about these, just stop for the time being, and return to the exploration at another time. This is another area where the guidance of a mental health professional could be of assistance.

Then too, building your self by initiating or enhancing your creativity, inspirational life, and relationships can also be of assistance in addition to the self-exploration. Chapters 9 and 10 provide some guidance and strategies for these.

THE MIRROR

This probably was not an easy chapter for you to read, but if you stuck with it you gained a considerable amount of information about self-absorption, and are to be commended. If you are open to even considering that you may have some underdeveloped narcissism, that too should be commended as that openness is a necessary condition for change. You may deny or reject having some self-absorbed behaviors and attitudes, and you may not, or the ones as described here don't seem to fit you. This may or may not be true, but, you don't have to accept this at this time. But, stay open to the possibility and learn more from others' feedback, and from your self-examination.

What can be especially revealing if you stay open to the possibility is how you mirror the self-absorbed behaviors and attitudes of your unsuitable lover. Before you reject any possibility that you too have a particular self-absorbed behavior or attitude, you could profit from staying open to that possibility, reflect on your behavior or attitude, and see the resemblance, although yours may differ in some level and kind. For example, he/she may be more obvious in attention-seeking behavior, and differ in actions from you, but your attention-seeking behavior still exists.

8

The Curious Rebel and the Exotic, Different, Unsuitable Lover

The attractiveness of the exotic, different, unsuitable lover lies primarily in your curiosity and rebelliousness. This lover probably has the following characteristics that you find alluring:

- Significantly different from your family, friends, and background
- Presents an air of the unknown that you find interesting and exciting
- Not ordinary, routine, or mundane
- Surrounded by glamour and/or mystery
- Presents you with a challenge
- Attracts attention, especially when you are with him/her

We'll discuss each of these attractions, but first it must be clearly stated that just being exotic and different does not equate with unsuitability. The unsuitability comes from having many or most of the characteristics described in the chapter on clear signs of unsuitability. The focus here is on your attraction to the exotic and different and how that attraction may lead you to make unwise choices—overlooking or ignoring signals of unsuitability.

Different

The attraction for you is that this person is different in significant and important ways from your family, friends, and others in your background. Although growing up in a homogenous community in the United States is becoming less prevalent, the personal associates for many people are still mainly homogenous around characteristics that are important to them. Take a look at your usual associates now, and during your developmental years. How diverse were they in race, ethnic group, religion, sexual identity and orientation, and/or socioeconomic status? As you became an adult, you could add the variables of education, occupation, marital status, and basic interests. There still may not be much diversity, except for your unsuitable lover. What made or contributed to your reaching out beyond the usual for this relationship? One or more of the following may have happened:

- Experienced betrayal and/or rejection
- Became disenchanted by the behavior of some people
- Desired strongly to show your independence from your parents
- Angry at parental demands for you, their actions, and/or feeling alienated from them
- Unable to accept human frailties about people you looked up to and admired
- Wanting to just get away
- Saw in the exotic and different something you wanted or admired

The very difference itself was attractive, and you were at a point or in a state where you wanted to do something new and exciting, or to get even with your parents, or were searching for something or someone who met your basic standards better than the people in your usual world. You may have felt confined, betrayed because people or religion or the like were not as you thought they should be, were hurting and looking for something to assuage that hurt, and other such reasons. You could not find what you wanted among the usual, so you decided to try the different.

It can be life-expanding and enhancing to get out of your comfort zone and interact with people who differ from you in significant ways. Getting to know them as individuals can do much to help you feel less threatened by differences, to understand their worlds, to learn to appreciate their culture, and to learn new ways of behaving and relating. Cross cultural and diversity sensitivity can be very rewarding, and is very necessary in today's world. There are many positive reasons for being open to other cultures and to diverse people, and this is encouraged. However, that does not mean that you have to tolerate behavior that you would not tolerate from people from your background, nor should you romanticize them just because they are different.

THE UNKNOWN

You may be attracted because you are intrigued by mystery and the unknown. Challenges to reveal and solve the mystery interest you. You like trying new, different, and exciting things whether those things are physical, emotional, cognitive, or spiritual. The unknown attracts you. Try the following exercise.

Exercise 8.1. My Interests

Materials: A sheet of paper and a pen or pencil for writing.
Procedure:

1. Sit in silence and let your thoughts go back to your childhood play, hobbies, recreational pursuits, and school subjects' interests.
2. Write childhood as a heading on the paper, and then list all of the activities that emerged as you completed step 1. They don't have to be in categories, just list them as they come to mind.

3. Sit again in silence and reflect on the same sort of activities, such as play, that engaged you during your adolescence.

4. Write adolescence as a heading and list all the activities that emerged as you reflected on these years.

5. Once again, sit in silence and think about your activities as an adult. The ones that capture your interests and/or fancy, and that you actively engage in doing on a pretty regular or consistent basis.

6. Review your lists for these three periods in your life and categorize each activity as one of the following:

I: Investigative
S: Social
C: Creative
CM: Competitive (such as card games, sports)
N: New or novel
CV: Conventional

7. Next, categorize each as one of the following intrigues, or satisfiers. That is, what do you recall as being pleasurable about the activity? More than one can apply, but try to identify the major one.

P: Physical
C: Cognitive
E: Emotional
I: Inspirational
S: Social connections

8. Review what you listed and categorized, and write a summary paragraph about your interests.

You may fall into either of two extremes. The first is that you were attracted by the mystery of the unknown and still seek out those challenges in parts of your life. The second is that you were and are somewhat conventional with an underlying desire to break out. Either extreme can contribute to your being attracted by the exotic and different.

Look behind the layer that makes the person you are attracted to appear exotic and different. That layer can be physical where there are visible differences that are appealing, or thoughts where the differences as they become known are challenging but also attractive, or activities that are new and novel for you, or whatever is exotic and different. What's beyond this layer? Does this person share your basic values and principles? These can transcend differences and form meaningful connections, but if not shared, can put you at a disadvantage and contribute to your forming a relationship with an unsuitable lover that is not mutually meaningful or satisfying.

NOT ORDINARY

The search for an antidote to ordinary, mundane, and routine can lead to making unwise choices in lovers because you are restless and dissatisfied, but do not understand what within you is producing this state. So, you look for external stimulation and get attracted to someone out of the ordinary for you, who seem exciting because they are not mundane or routine, and you never examine your inner self for the source of your restlessness, or seek differences for other parts of your self or your life. There are so many things you could do to curb your restlessness and even boredom that would not result in establishing a relationship with an unsuitable lover.

This restlessness can emerge even if you are very busy and active. Just look at what is written or shown on television about sports figures, entertainment figures, politicians, and the like and you will see that many of them are very involved and active, but still leap from person to person, event to event, new activity to new activity almost constantly. They seem restless, easily bored, and distracted, and don't appear to be centered, grounded, with a strong sense of self. So, you can become restless and bored even when being bombarded with external stimuli. These don't seem to fit, hit the mark, or satisfy. That's because the real is within that person.

Think about a time when you were feeling restless, and reflect on the following questions:

- Were you counting on external sources to be stimulating and/or satisfying and this was not happening?
- What part of your life was satisfying? What part was not?
- Were you living up to your expectations for yourself in all aspects of your life such as work, status, relationships, financial, and so on? Or was there one or more aspects where you were failing, being thwarted, or wanted out?
- Did you engage in altruistic acts where you gave of yourself without any strings or expectations?
- Or was your giving in an expectation of receiving in return or had conditions attached?
- Was there turmoil in your life, depression, or vague dissatisfaction that was difficult to identify or pin down?
- Did you try to figure out why you felt as you did, but only became frustrated?

You may want to try writing your answers, and then analyzing them to see how you looked outside your self for stimulation and answers and did not do sufficient self-examination to better understand the underlying causes for your restlessness.

Many people who are restless do look outside their selves for relief, but may fail to realize that this leaves them open and vulnerable to doing things that are not in their best interests, and/or getting in relationships that lead to undesirable results. If this description fits you, the next time you are aware of your restlessness or boredom, stop and reflect on what within you is promoting the dissatisfaction with oneself. Work on this before looking for external sources to relieve the dissatisfaction and/or boredom. While a change could make a difference, be careful about changes you make when you are in this state as these may not be carefully examined before adoption.

GLAMOUR

Glamour is by definition dazzling, enticing, romantic, and is surrounded by excitement. It can be easy to get caught up in the appearances and not be able to see beyond that, or to realize the effects glamour is having on you. You can definitely be wearing "rose-colored glasses" where everything negative is filtered out, and you see only what you want to see.

The exotic, different, unsuitable lover may appeal to you because of your definition of glamour. He/she appears glamorous and you are dazzled, excited, and want to be included in his/her world. You may even think, on some level, that this association makes you appear more glamorous, which could also be one of your attractors.

You may think that glamorous people get attention, admiration, preferential treatment, and are "bigger than life." Some of this is certainly true some of the time, but the bigger question may be why you are attracted. Is it because you want what they have? Or, is it because you are similar in some important ways? Or, are you longing to be different than you are? The answers to these could provide meaningful insights that are helpful for self-understanding.

Some measure of the dazzle, romance, and excitement could be pleasurable but hard to sustain on a regular basis. I would suggest that large and continuous doses lead to stress which can have negative effects on your physical, mental, relational, and emotional well-being, although when experienced on a short-term basis can be stimulating and satisfying. A balance is preferable.

So, just being glamorous is not being unsuitable, but the glamour is your attraction to the person. What happens when the glamour fades? Does the attraction also fade? Was your attraction only to the surface glamour? If so, what does that tell you about your needs, values, and the like? You may want to reflect on the extent to which you are being superficial, unauthentic, and looking for reflected admiration and attention from association with the glamorous person.

Meaningful, satisfying, and enduring relationships need more than superficiality. Until you can identify what glamour attracts you, and why you want this, you will not make much headway on eliminating relationships with unsuitable lovers. Try the following scale to identify your glamour attractors.

Exercise 8.2. My Glamour Attractors

Directions:

1. Rate the extent to which you think each item conveys glamour using the following scale. The second step is presented after this list of items.

    5: Extremely descriptive of glamour
    4: Very descriptive of glamour
    3: Somewhat descriptive of glamour
    2: Little descriptive of glamour
    1: Not at all descriptive of glamour

    a. Fun
    b. Excitement
    c. Attracts envy
    d. Others get jealous
    e. Attracts admiration
    f. Does extraordinary things
    g. Grand, heroic
    h. Can ignore convention
    i. Desirable, arouses lust
    j. Receives deference

Scoring: Add your ratings to derive a total score.

2. Now, think of a person to whom you are attracted in a current intimate relationship, or someone from a past intimate relationship. Rate that person on each item.

Scoring: Add your scores to derive a total score.

3. Compare the two scores for similarity, that is, how close are the total ratings. The closer the ratings, the more the real person meets your idea of glamour.

Presents a Challenge

What's your initial reaction when someone says any of the following to you?

- Don't do that
- You can't do that
- You better stop doing that
- You'll get in trouble if you do that

If you are honest and your response is some version of digging your heels in and becoming stubborn, then you really rise to a challenge. Your competitive spirit kicks in and you devise ways to do and get what others seem to be denying you. You are out to prove them wrong, and to show them that you can do it.

Some of this competitive spirit plays into your decision to choose the exotic, different, unsuitable lover. No one has to openly or directly challenge you; this is something you do for yourself. But, if someone were to suggest that hooking up with this person was not a good idea, you would probably see that as a challenge to prove them wrong. You may not openly agree, but in your mind you're saying, "We'll just see about that."

This sort of competitive spirit is what has produced inventions, created new processes, accumulated fortunes, motivated adventures, and led to new discoveries. Where channeled in appropriate ways, and on appropriate targets, this spirit can accomplish some wonderful things. You may want to keep this in mind the next time you feel you must rise to a challenge, and be a little more discriminating about your choices of action just to prove the other person as wrong.

It could be helpful for you to not react immediately to a challenge, but to take some time to think it through and weigh the pros and cons of proceeding to address the challenge, especially so if you have not succeeded in that part. That failure could be a sign that some challenges are best left where they are, and your energies and efforts employed in more fruitful pursuits. In other words, you don't have to let your competitive spirit galvanize you into doing foolish things or making unwise choices. You can take charge, and make decisions about which challenges would be worthwhile to pursue, and which ones are not.

Stopping to think it through could be especially beneficial in the case with intimate relationships with exotic different people. On some level, you may be responding to an unspoken message not to do that, and your characteristic response of, "I'll do it if I want to." When you are inclined to ignore such a message because you don't like being told what or what not to do, that's the time to try and examine your characteristic response for its validity for this circumstance. In other words, you are not trying to ignore or change your response; you are maturely examining it for the particular circumstance. You don't have to give up your competitive spirit, or cave in to others' dictates, you are analyzing the situation and your desires to make better and more informed choices.

Choosing an exotic different lover because you respond to a challenge is not beneficial for either of you. That can devalue and demean the other person even if you never openly admit this. Peoples' affections are not trophies to be won over by others, they are best when freely given. You will want to carefully examine your reasons for desiring this exotic different person so that both of you will benefit from the relationship if he/she is suitable in other respects.

When your competitive spirit gets aroused, you can stop and reflect on the following questions. The answers can help you decide if this challenge is worth your time and effort.

- Am I just being stubborn because I don't like being told what, or what not to do?
- Do I think or feel that this nay sayer is telling me that I'm not good enough
- Have I considered the feelings of the other person(s) who may be affected by what I do?
- What will I win, accomplish, or achieve by following through on this challenge?
- Is this worth the time and effort I'll have to expend?
- What might be a better use of my time and resources?
- How do I think I will feel if I were to succeed?

ATTRACTS ATTENTION

You may like having heads turn and other kinds of attention you attract when you are with an exotic different person and this makes you feel special, unique, desirable, and so on. On the other side, if you are in a community where being seen with someone like this brings disapproval, you may like that negative response and want to rub their noses in it. This is the revenge motive, and is more about your relationships with parents, friends, and others in your community than it is about the exotic different person.

Another possible reason is that you like the attention that person receives, and/or that the two of you receive when appearing together. You don't get this reception when you are alone or with someone from your usual background and feel more excited and alive when you get this attention, you enjoy the feeling of being perceived as special, unique, exciting, and so on. You can even project that others are envious of you being with this person.

There is an additional reason why you choose an exotic different lover who attracts attention; you are making a point to be visible to the world that you are open and accepting of others who are different from you in important ways. And, that you are not biased or prejudiced, you are carrying a message that you reject those concepts and acts, and you want everyone to know this. While this is certainly a laudable position to not be biased as prejudiced, you may want to reflect on how you may be using this person to fulfill your personal needs, and are not attracted to him/her as he/she really is.

How does this attention make you feel? Take a moment to reflect on the feelings that emerge when you and the exotic different lover attract attention, and write a list of the various feelings you experience. You may have some of the following:

- Satisfaction at standing out from the crowd
- Reassurance that you exist
- Exultation at winning over others
- Delight at one-upmanship
- Glory for showing off
- Pleasure for being powerful

If you notice, these feelings are all about you, and this can be a signal that your motives are about some basic and personal issues and concerns, and that this is the way that you have chosen to handle them, you may need to engage in some self-exploration to get a better understanding of your underlying issues so as to fulfill these in a more positive and satisfying way. This too may be a work that needs the guidance of a competent mental health professional. Understanding can assist you to make better choices, and to be able to see beyond the exoticism and difference so that you stop selecting this type of unsuitable lover.

You may also want to consider getting your attention in more constructive ways, and to decide how much attention you want.

Exercise 8.3. Get Attention

Materials: A sheet of paper and a pen or pencil for writing.
Procedure:

1. Find a place to work where you will not be disturbed.
2. Make a list of actions or activities that bring or that brought you desired attention, beginning in childhood.

3. Rate each of these on a scale from 0 (not satisfying) to 10 (extremely satisfying).
4. Write the kind of audience that provides the attention beside each item on the list.
5. Review your list, ratings, and audience and see if a pattern emerges that captures the activities that bring the most satisfying attention. Make a new list of these.
6. Using the new list, identify the motive that gets satisfied by the activity as power, affection, control, revenge, approval, or reassurance.
7. Reflect on your most frequent motive and think of two or three new constructive actions or activities that may also satisfy your motive to get attention.
8. Resolve to implement one or more of these in the next two weeks.

By now you are more aware of some of your needs, characteristics, and desires that may be fueling your tendency to choose exotic and different unsuitable lovers, and you have some suggestions for self-exploration for deeper understanding and some specific suggestions for making changes that may help in making future decisions, hopefully more positive ones, about lovers. Let's take a look at the two major reasons for your attraction to exotic, different, unsuitable lovers: curiosity and rebelliousness.

CURIOSITY

Being curious and wanting to know about the unknown can be positive attributes and are definite requirements for some careers such as medical researchers, scientists, engineers, criminal investigation, and financial auditors. Even some of those who are attracted to artistic and social careers can also have these characteristics, and scholars in every field must have these. Your curiosity vent could be very positive for you if channeled correctly.

These characteristics are not very positive or helpful when used in ways that intentionally or unintentionally exploit or hurt others or that have these possibilities. Examples for this include ferreting out personal secrets and revealing these such as what can happen with gossip, meddling in others' affairs, and forming relationships just to find out about the other person. Curiosity, in these instances, can be malicious and certainly is not constructive. Your need to know is not respectful of the other person's rights as a separate and distinct individual who has value and worth.

When you combine your natural characteristic of curiosity with an insensitivity to others, you can then become relentless in your zeal to satisfy the curiosity and ignore the other person's rights. There may be an unconscious assumption on your part that you have a right to use this person for your needs. This may be what fuels your movement into the unsuitable relationship.

You may be thinking that the exotic, different, unsuitable lovers are the seducers and aggressors, that you were too naïve and trusting, and this is a reason why you keep making the unsuitable choices. Indeed, you may be correct to a point. You may have insufficient boundary strength, be looking for admiration and approval, and lack a self-understanding that would enable you to withstand seduction and aggression by others. But, you are likely to also have the curiosity that allows you to be open and receptive. Think about it. Why did this person pick you to seduce? Since you've come to know of their unsuitability, why wasn't this apparent from the beginning of the relationship? Why did you persist after the first stirrings of discomfort about the relationship? The answers to these, and other questions, lie within and about you. These exotic different lovers are as they are, and you cannot change them. You can best understand and build your self so that you can better resist seduction and aggression.

What may be helpful for you to try is to become more detached and cognitive about the object(s) of your curiosity. Stay intensely interested and seek out knowledge and understanding like the scientists and scholars do, but be less inclined to become so emotionally involved that you lose your sense of self as separate and distinct. It is easier to be detached and cognitive about abstractions and ideas, but much less so about relationships of any kind, so this maybe difficult for you to do. This can be especially difficult when there is a strong physical component for the attraction as that can interfere with thinking. Cognitive strategies are presented in Chapters 9 and 10, but here is an exercise that you can try to begin this process.

Exercise 8.4. Detaching

Materials: Several sheets of paper, pen or pencil, and crayons or felt markers or colored pencils.
Procedure:

1. Find a place to work that has a suitable writing surface (a large book can suffice for this), and where you will not be disturbed.
2. Sit in silence, close your eyes, and recall the first time you saw or met one of your exotic, different, unsuitable lovers. Try to recall as much about the environment, activity taking place, feelings you experienced, and so on. Take as long as you like for this step.
3. When you have fully immersed yourself in the recall, let the images emerge that seem to capture the essence of the whole event. Do not edit, evaluate, or change the image(s), just let it (them) emerge.
4. Use the crayons, or felt markers, or colored pencils to draw the images. These can be realistic, abstract, metaphors (something that wasn't present at that time, but did emerge as an image), or just the feelings that you experienced. Be as fanciful as you like.
5. When you are finished with your image drawing, sit in silence once again, and reflect on your drawing.
6. Select another sheet of paper and write a summary paragraph about your drawing. What does it depict? What do the images portray? What feelings do you have as you look at your picture? Are these intense, or mild, or just interesting?

What can happen as you think and imagine is that you become less emotionally involved. Your energy goes to noticing details and finding words, and there is less energy focused on your feelings. This gives you time to think about what you are experiencing, to evaluate its impact and potential for you, and to make a more informed judgment or decision instead of acting on an impulse. Try the same exercise for the first time you dated or spent time with the unsuitable lover and see what emerges that you did not notice at the time, both for what you felt and what you thought.

In the future, you can use steps 1–3 to detach when you encounter or are attracted to someone. You don't have to close your eyes as the imaging and thinking can also be effectively done with your eyes open. Thinking before you act can help prevent you from becoming intimately involved with unsuitable lovers.

POSITIVE REBELLION

Like so many other actions, rebellion can be both positive and negative. If used constructively, it can keep you from blind acceptance of conventional thinking and acting, expand your horizons, discover new things, enhance creativity, and a whole host of other positive outcomes. Rebellion for rebellion's sake is immature and does nothing constructive for anyone. Rebellion that has revenge as a motive, for real or imagined injury, is also negative and can be destructive. So, if you deliberately seek out and establish relationships with exotic different lovers (unsuitable or suitable ones), because you are rebelling for any reason, you may find that it is much more constructive to channel your rebellion in more positive ways, and to not use others, to achieve your goals as this is exploitation.

How can you make your rebellion positive? The following steps describe a process for evaluating your rebellion. You can write your answers, or just think it through, but you have to be honest with yourself or the process will not produce the desirable outcome.

1. What specifically are you rebelling against? You need to be able to clearly state this. Behavioral descriptions are best rather than things like an attitude.
2. Describe examples of what fuels your rebellion such as words or actions of others.
3. List the feelings that are aroused in you when you encounter what you are rebelling against; feelings such as helpless, impotent, devalued and the, like. Anger is a given, but beneath the anger are other feelings.
4. Think about and try to identify what may be triggering and fueling the behavior for that person, or those persons, that leads to your rebellion. Could it be a need for power or control, fear, a search for certainty, or something similar to these?
5. Now, try to gauge the quality and strength of the relationship they have with you. Give the relationship a rating from 0 (little or no quality or strength) to 10 (an extremely important and quality relationship).

6. Rate the degree of influence and impact these people, or this person, have on your current life. Use a rating from 0 (little or no influence or impact) to 10 (an extreme influence and impact). (Note: you may want to judge if the influence and impact are objectively realistic if your rating is 2 or above.)

7. If your rating is 5 or below, ask yourself why you continue to respond to someone who isn't being important for your world at this time. Ratings above 5 need consideration about your degree of separation and individuation with this person, or with these people. You may still be reacting to them as you did when you were younger, and not based on your current status as an adult.

You may want to take some time to reflect on your need to continue rebelling against people who have little or no influence and impact on your adult life, or continuing to respond as an adult like you did when you were a child or an adolescent. At any rate, you are now in a better position to choose whether or not to rebel, and can make more adult discussions about how to rebel. You don't have to reject everything about them, your relationship with them, or do what's best for you even if that something appears to be in line with their expectations, demands, and wishes. You are an adult and can choose what's best for you.

Let's turn attention to ways you can make your rebellion more positive. The first step would be to identify why you feel a need to rebel. Some possible reasons include the following:

- You don't like them and want to show that dislike
- You want to prove them wrong and show your superiority at being right
- You want to arouse their anger and/or fear
- You want to hurt them
- You are seeking to assert your autonomy
- You just want to try something new

Embedded in these reasons is also the condition that they must be aware of your rebellion and hopefully, powerless to prevent it. They must also have a strong reaction to the rebellion, and/or understand the message you are sending them.

Ask yourself the following questions about your reason(s) for rebelling:

- Why is it so important for someone to know you don't like them that you do things to emphasize the dislike?
- If you are superior and/or right, will that not emerge and be seen without extra effort?
- What are you vengeful about? How did they hurt you? Do this desire and action of revenge suggest that you are like them? Wouldn't it be more positive for you to heal your hurt?
- Can you be autonomous and assertive because that's what you want, and not because you need to rebel?
- Are you able to try something new on your own, or are you unconsciously seeking approval to do so?

More positive attitudes would not have a revenge motive, or a need to show your superiority and others' inferiority. You would not be trying to upset anyone, you are simply doing what you feel is right for you, making informed decisions and choices, and seeking self-improvement. You can be different, do different things, reject what does not fit you, and embrace new ways without the negative motives. This is another reason why it is important that you be clear in your mind why you are seeking a relationship with an exotic different person. It is much more positive to be doing so because you have freely chosen to do so without negative motives such as those that can accompany rebellion.

Positive rebellion could be about rejecting the following attitudes and behaviors:

- Stereotyping, bias, and prejudice
- Categorizing and responding to people on the basis of socioeconomic status
- Disdain for poor people
- Aversion to people with disabilities
- Gender, age, sexual orientation, racial/ethnic, and religious discriminatory acts
- Social injustice
- Acceptance of immoral, illegal, and/or unethical behavior
- Emotional and/or physical abuse
- Attitudes that encourage manipulation, seduction, unfair treatment, cheating, and the like

You can probably add more to this list.

BRING EXOTICISM AND DIFFERENCE INTO YOUR LIFE

You don't have to look to another person for exoticism and difference. If you want to interrupt the routine, feel energized and interested, explore the new and novel, or reveal the mystery, you have other avenues and resources you can use. You may want to discover and try these as antidotes to continuing to choose exotic and different unsuitable lovers.

Understanding some of your motives, such as restlessness and curiosity, can assist in selecting other avenues and resources. Complete the following exercise to get started thinking about these as they would best fit you.

Exercise 8.5. My Motives

Materials: A sheet of paper, and a pen or pencil.
Procedure:

1. Find a place to work where you will not be disturbed, and that has a suitable surface for writing.
2. Rate how important each of the following is as a motive for your actions, especially when choosing an exotic different person for a relationship.

0: No importance
1: Little importance
2: Some importance
3: Important
4: Very important
5: Extremely important

- Restlessness
- Excitement
- Rebellion
- Curiosity
- Challenge

3. Select the motive with the highest rating and list two to three activities that you've used successfully in the past, other than a person.
4. Repeat step 3 for each of the other motives, except those you rated 0 or 1.
5. You should now have a list of alternatives for your motives.

If you feel your list is too short, or you would like other ideas, consider the following as possibilities:

Restlessness: Volunteer activities that help others (recreation, sports, dance or other physical activities)

Excitement: Discover a new idea, read for vicarious excitement, explore your inner self and reveal new information

Rebellion: Volunteer at a soup kitchen, work on a political campaign, meditate daily

Curiosity: Take a class, organize treasure hunts, learn to fix something or how something works

Challenge: Take up a new endeavor such as gourmet cooking, event planning, or hang gliding

Whatever you think of as exotic and different can be brought into your life without exploiting someone, rebelling in negative way, or making unwise choices for lovers.

9

REDUCE SUSCEPTIBILITY AND BUILD RESISTANCE

Reducing your susceptibility involves strengthening your psychological boundary strength so that you don't become involuntarily enmeshed, overwhelmed, seduced, and so on. You are able to make informed choices that hopefully do not get you entangled with unsuitable lovers. You pay too high a cost for those relationships and receive nothing in return that is of lasting value, except not to repeat the experience. Even that does not work and you can and do find yourself in the same kind of unproductive relationship over and over again, and this plays havoc with your self-esteem, self-confidence, and your emotional and even your physical well-being. There are many positive outcomes for reducing your susceptibility and building your resistance. This chapter presents suggestions and strategies for both.

The extent of your emotional susceptibility is dependent on the strength of your psychological boundaries that define you as separate and distinct from others. Psychological boundary strength is hard to define and describe; some of it is hidden as you act on your unconscious fantasies, old parental messages, and repressed memories and feelings but are not consciously aware of doing this; it is dependent on your growth and development during your formative years; and you can remain unaware of its strength or lack of strength. So, how does one go about recognizing and building something that is so vague and nebulous? The following can begin the process, but you must realize that it is a long unfolding process that can continue over a lifetime as more and more hidden aspects of self become apparent to you, and some work may need to be done with the help of a competent therapist. Some identifiers can include the following:

- The extent of longing for approval, liking, and acceptance
- Anxiety and feeling responsible for others' welfare even when they are capable adults
- Responsiveness to others' wishes, demands, and the like
- Ease of access to guilt and shame for disappointing others

- Failure to recognize others' physical, emotional, and/or psychological boundaries
- Overidentification with others' emotions, problems, and concerns, and taking these on as yours
- The inability to say no, and/or to stick with your decision in the face of others' persuasion or insistence
- Pervasive and extensive fear of being alone
- Yearning and longing for parental love approval, and empathy that is not forthcoming
- Lack of awareness about your emotional triggers

Longing for Approval, Liking, and Acceptance

You can estimate the extent to which you long for the approval, liking, and acceptance by others by reflecting on these questions.

- What are you willing to do to get these from others?
- How much of your self are you willing to compromise to be like others want you to be, even if that's not constructive or right for you?
- How often do you neglect, ignore, or compromise your values, principles, and the like because you want someone to like, approve, and accept you?
- Do you feel more secure when someone indicates his/her liking, approval, and/or acceptance of you, and feel that you must do something to gain these when they are not immediately forthcoming?
- When do you most like, approve of, and accept yourself?

If your answers are somewhat disquieting, then you feel it is extremely or very important to have others approve, like, and accept you, and you may be doing things you don't want to, or that are not in your best interests, just to get these. This need helps to keep you susceptible to the attraction to unsuitable lovers, and maybe other unsavory characters who exploit and manipulate you for their benefit.

Reducing or eliminating this longing is a long-term activity that calls for self-exploration, an understanding of one's course of personal development, in addition to a commitment for change. You may need the guidance of a mental health professional to effectively guide your self-exploration, understanding, and change as these are very complex. However, these are strategies you can employ until this work is done that may be helpful:

- Focus on the other person and stay aware of your liking, approval, and acceptance of him/her instead of wondering how he/she feels about you.
- Ask yourself, "What do I want to do before agreeing to do what someone else wants, and be willing to stick to my answer for this?"
- Ask yourself, "What do I most fear will happen if I don't get this person's approval, liking, or acceptance? What do I lose? Can I pay this price?"
- Reflect each day on three things you did that merit your approval, another three things that you like about yourself, and three self-accepting thoughts and attitudes. You may find it helpful to do this each day for a month, and to record these.

RESPONSIBLE FOR OTHERS' WELFARE

Your susceptibility can be more easily triggered if you feel you are responsible for others' welfare, and this feeling can extend to adults who should be able to attend to their own welfare. Let's back up just a little and say that caring about the welfare of others is a positive characteristic, and that we need more of this in the world. Simply caring about others' welfare is not the problem. You may do more than care; you may think that it is your responsibility to make sure that they do not experience distress, discomfort, disappointment, disharmony, or other similar things. That's where caring goes too far, becomes counterproductive for you, and leaves you vulnerable to seduction, manipulation, and exploitation.

You may be responding, in part, to old parental messages that made you responsible for one or more parent's emotional well-being, or childhood teachings that told you that you were guilty or shameful for not preventing others' distress and so on. You internalized one or both of these, and are now still acting on them as an adult. Thus, your thoughts, beliefs, attitudes, and feelings about the extent of your duty and obligations to others are a major contributor to your susceptibility.

This illogical thought of yours plays into the hands of anyone who wants to manipulate and exploit you because all they have to do to arouse your guilt is to act or suggest that you are not fulfilling the expectations they have for you, or that they are disappointed with you, and so on. You may be so sensitive and responsive to others' welfare needs that you act to prevent them from possible distress, they don't even have to say or ask anything. You try to anticipate their needs and give it to them. You don't want to feel inadequate or guilty.

Changing this thought for you will require some time and effort because it's not just a behavior or thought susceptible to will-power. These are also deep-seated, long-standing feelings about one's self involved, and these can be difficult to overcome. It's a pattern and conviction established early in life, and help may be needed to begin to let others have the responsibility to care for themselves and to let go of guilt feelings for not attending to their welfare. In the meantime, you can use the following to help reduce this behavior and the accompanying feelings:

Suggestion: *Whenever you think you must act to take care of a functional adult's wants, wishes, desires, or needs, stop and reflect on the extent of your responsibility for this. Reflect also on the fact that they are also responsible for their feelings, just as you are responsible for your feelings. Another reflection as part of this process is to ask yourself the following questions: What do you want to do? Is the request or expectation in your best interest? Is the person attempting to manipulate and exploit you?*

GUILT AND SHAME

Triggering your guilt and/or shame can almost always be counted on to get you to act to reduce or eliminate these feelings. Only amoral people don't experience these feelings and seem to have no moral compass that recognizes the existences or rights of others. So, not being amoral can leave you vulnerable to experiencing guilt and shame.

Guilt is formed when we fail to meet standards for right and moral behavior, acting in accord with values and principles, and for disappointing self and others. So, the desire is to make up or atone for these, to recapture the feeling that the self is moral, ethical, valuable, and worthwhile, and that you meet all expectations you have for your self. You may not have given thought to identifying where these personal standards, values, and principles, and the conviction that you must meet others' expectations came from, how you developed and internalized these, if these meet your needs and are worth keeping as part of you, or how they impact your life. These would be worthy explorations whose answers may have the effect of reducing guilt feelings, or at least narrowing these so that they become less troublesome and have less of a negative impact on your vulnerability.

Shame is triggered when you fear that your self is fatally flawed, and when others see these flaws, you will be destroyed. The flaws are so great and are impossible to fix that the self should not be allowed to exist. Think of how you feel when you experience any of the following which are variations for shame:

- Embarrassment
- Chagrin
- Regret or remorse
- Humiliation

Many people just want to get away, hide, and not be seen by those who witnessed the act that produced the feeling.

You produce your feeling of shame even when others may be telling you that you should or ought to feel that. You feel shamed because others can now see your inadequacies and flaws that you were trying to hide, suppress, repress, or deny. You can feel exposed and vulnerable, and this can be intensified if you are the kind of person that is very sensitive to what others think about you. You aren't accepting of your self, and don't expect that others can accept you either. This status makes you open and susceptible to manipulation and exploitation as you are in a position where you are willing to go to extremes to keep the shameful self from being seen.

Shame is also developed, as is guilt, and it is deep and long standing. What produces shame for you can come from old parental messages that were incorporated and acted on without neither conscious examination nor examined today as an adult, conscious and unconscious messages from significant people during your formative years, the prevailing standards for your community, and now, even from the media and global communities. Your self-concept and self-acceptance were shaped by many forces, but the strongest ones tend to be the early experiences from your family of origin.

Reducing triggered shame involves becoming more self-accepting. This is not an easy task, and like most everyone else there may be parts of your self that you feel need changing to become more acceptable to you. This too is long term and involves personal work. In the short term you can try the following:

Suggestion: *Emphasize your strengths when you think about your self. Focus more on what you are that you approve of, what you do well that pleases you, and progress you make on desired changes. It can also be helpful to tell yourself that you will do better next time when you make a mistake that leads to feelings of embarrassment, chagrin, regret or remorse, shame, or humiliation.*

FAILURE TO RECOGNIZE BOUNDARIES

Part of learning that one's self is separate and distinct from others is the recognition of others' physical, emotional, and psychological boundaries. That is, where you end, and where others begin. When your boundaries are firmly established in your mind, you become much less vulnerable and susceptible to others' manipulation and exploitation. This recognition of boundaries is a process called separation and individuation that begins in childhood and continues throughout life. To get an idea of how much you may be unconsciously violating others' boundaries, try the following exercise:

Exercise 9.1. Boundary Violations

Directions: Reflect on your usual behavior with people closest to you such as family including children, friends, and extended family if you have frequent contact and/or interaction with them. Use the following scale to rate yourself:

5: Always or almost always
4: Very often
3: Frequently or usually
2: Infrequently or seldom
1: Never or almost never

1. Borrow or use possessions without first obtaining the owner's permission.
2. Hugging, patting, or some form of touching others because you want to.
3. Asking personal questions that are intrusive and expecting answers.
4. Become irritated or taken aback when someone doesn't want to answer your questions.
5. Expect others to tell you what they are thinking or feeling without your having to ask.
6. Expect others to tell you what they are thinking or feeling when you ask, and become annoyed or hurt when they do not.
7. Frequent phone calls during the day and you expect him/her to answer.
8. Others' plans should be always presented to you for your approval, consent, and the like.

9. Volunteer others' time, resources, and so on, without first asking them.
10. Accept invitations and the like without first confirming what the other person(s) want to do.

Scoring: Add your ratings to derive a total score, and use the following to guide your interpretation:

41–50: There are a considerable number of boundary violations that may be unconscious, and you may not be aware or sensitive to the impact on others.
31–40: There are many boundary violations, but you are not paying attention to the impact of these on others.
21–30: You violate others' boundaries some of the time. Examine your responses to see if the most frequent violations are for physical, emotional, or psychological boundaries.
10–20: You do violate others' boundaries on occasions.
0–9: You are sensitive to others' boundaries and seldom, if ever, violate these.

Ten Strategies to Reduce Your Violations of Others' Boundaries

1. Ask others' permission before borrowing their possessions. This also applies to children.
2. Ask before touching, such as saying, "Can I give you a hug?"
3. Refrain from asking personal questions of any type. Allow others to tell you when *they* are ready.
4. If you do #3, that can help reduce the number of times you can become irritated or taken aback. When you do have this (these) feeling(s), remind yourself that the other person has a right to privacy, and that you do not have a right to intrude.
5. You may want to examine the feelings you experience when someone doesn't tell you what he/she is experiencing without you having to ask. These are likely to be irrational and can negatively impact the relationship. You do not have any right to know this about the other, even if you tend to be more forthcoming about your thoughts and feelings. Show confidence in the relationship and in the other person by being comfortable with what he/she shares, and not fretting or suspicious about what isn't shared.
6. If you ask and the other person doesn't satisfactorily answer the way you want them to, back off and let them alone. Pushing or demanding information he/she doesn't want to share puts a strain on the relationship, makes it appear that you don't trust him/her, and is intrusive. That person has a right to privacy.
7. You are intruding into the other person's life when you do this, unless it is mutually agreeable. Examine your need for constant contact.
8. This is another situation where there needs to be mutual agreement. But, needing to know everything is an attempt to be controlling and can be corrosive to every relationship. Some plans need to be shared, but not all of them.
9. Speak only for yourself, and let others speak for themselves.
10. Make it a practice to check with the other person before making any commitments that involve him/her.

When you can recognize others' boundaries, you more firmly establish your own. Your increased sensitivity to others can also increase your awareness and sensitivity to your self, and that is helpful to reduce your emotional suscepti-bility. All of these become helpful in your journey to becoming resistant to the lures, manipulation, and exploitation by unsuitable lovers.

OVERIDENTIFICATION

Weak, or spongy psychological boundaries permit you to "catch" others' feelings. But after taking these in, you can overidentify with them and start to feel as if their feelings, problems, or concerns are yours, and have a notion or conviction that it is your responsibility to fix these, solve problems, and soothe feelings. You don't recognize what is happening at the time, and may never recognize what happened.

Your tendency to overidentify can make you vulnerable to taking on others' unspoken and even unconscious needs, wishes, and desires to try and do something about them, and this can lead you to making unwise and foolish choices about people, relationships, and decisions about activities that are not in your best interest. You get all caught up in their stuff to the point where you fail to think things through, and end up somewhere you never intended to be. Your time and efforts as well as your thoughts and feelings, are consumed with making things better for the other person, and you neglect yourself.

What leads to insufficient boundary strength that allows you to overidentify? This state is probably not anything new for you, and you may have been doing it all your life. Even if you became aware of what you were doing at some point, and tried to stop, you had little or no success. This lack of success to change your behavior points out just how difficult this is, and that willpower alone is insufficient. Since your capture and overidentification usually happen on an unconscious level, you may not be successful at preventing capture and overidentification until you better understand your psychological development, and strengthen your psychological boundaries.

Central to your future growth and development of strong and resilient boundaries is your understanding about your early relationship with your par-ent(s), other family of origin experiences, and other past influential experiences. Since these were unique for you as they are for everyone, it is not possible to define these for you. But, there are some possibilities that may fit.

- Did you grow up in a home where one or more parents was very depressed?
- Did a parent make you responsible for his/her emotional well-being?
- Was there neglect or abuse for you during your formative years?
- Was it your responsibility to insure harmony, mediate conflicts, and so on?
- Were you given major responsibility for one or more siblings?
- Were you encouraged or expected to be "sweet" and suppress your needs, wishes, and desires for those of others?

- Does one or more of your parents (stepparents too) fill the description for a destructive narcissistic pattern? (See Chapter 7 on the self-absorbed unsuitable lover.)

These are a few possibilities for why you developed a tendency to overidentify. To change this tendency you have to first become aware of what captures you and initiate steps to strengthen your boundaries, and/or develop barriers. The next step is to better understand your inner experiencing that produces the overidentification so that if something does get through you don't become so closely identified with it that you take it as your own. This last step is much harder to do, and may need the guidance of a competent mental health professional. But, here are a few short-term strategies you can use until that work is fruitful.

1. Restrict your nonverbal behaviors that signal interest, intimacy, and caring to those whom you can trust because of past experiences with these particular people. The restriction would be in effect until any new person has proven himself/herself worthy of your trust. Behaviors that should be restricted include the following:
   - Turning your body to face the person
   - Sustained eye contact
   - Invasion of your personal space such as standing or sitting too close
   - Touching, such as patting, hugs, and so on
   - Hanging on his/her every word. Listen, but not this intently
   - Trying to empathize
2. Institute some emotional insulation when you find that your feelings are becoming intense so as to prevent further intensification where you can become enmeshed, mired, or overwhelmed by taking in and taking on others' feelings. Another time when emotional insulation would be helpful is when you sense that someone is trying to manipulate you. To institute emotional insulation, mentally think of and visualize some barrier between you and the other person. Barriers such as a wall, steel doors, a force field, or anything that would prevent you from catching someone's feelings can work. Use this technique frequently until you don't have to make a conscious effort to initiate it.
3. Remind yourself of the following every time you think you have to intervene for someone else:
   - I don't have to "fix it" unless asked, and I agree there are limits to my responsibility for other capable adults
   - Others have capabilities and resources to address their problems or concerns
   - I must respect others' abilities to care for themselves
   - It's not my problem or my responsibility
   - MMOB: I need to mind my own business

DIFFICULTY IN SAYING NO

Some people can have great difficulty first in saying no, and second in sticking to that decision. If this fits you, then you are extremely vulnerable to others' manipulation and exploitation. You probably feel that others routinely take advantage of your "good nature," and know that they can count on you. You also can experience some wishes to be different and able to say no sometimes, and also wish that you could stick to that decision but all too often you are cajoled, persuaded, flattered, have your guilt and/or shame triggered because of an unrealistic and exaggerated sense of responsibility, or manipulated to back off the no, and do whatever it was that you were refusing to do.

You probably experience one or more of the following when you want to say no:

- Apprehension about offending
- Fear of becoming rejected and abandoned
- Guilt for disappointing the person
- His/her approval and liking will be withdrawn
- You will be perceived as inadequate
- You will lose the relationship
- Failure to meet others' needs and expectations and that is indicative of your flaws

Rather than experience these negative feelings, you capitulate and retract the no. You don't feel good either way, but you feel less bad giving in.

These feelings are significant contributors to your inability to say no, and/or to stick with it. Most all of these, if not all of them, developed early in your life where you either did not have an option to say no, or were punished for not being agreeable and cooperative, or you tried very hard to please and not refusing anything someone wanted of you got you the approval you wanted and needed. You are probably still acting on the early experiences even as an adult.

Take another look at the possible reasons for your inability to say no and stick with it. Whatever your personal reason or reasons may be, they are leaving you vulnerable to seduction, manipulation, exploitation, and even control by others, and this may be especially so for unsuitable lovers. You are not going to be very successful at fending off unsuitable lovers until you resolve or solve your negative feelings that get aroused when you do try to say no and then stick to it. You fear and dread the consequences so much that you leave yourself open for all kinds of manipulation and exploitation. The personal work suggested for other behaviors and characteristics will assist also with this one. For the short term, you can try the following:

Exercise 9.2. Say No

Materials: One or more sheets of paper, pen or pencil, a mirror $9'' \times 12''$ or larger, and a tape recorder.
Procedure:

1. Find a place to work where you will not be interrupted, and that has a suitable writing surface.

2. Close your eyes and think of a situation you had where you wanted to say no, but did not, or where you did say no, but backed off. Try to remember as many details as possible about the other person, and about what you were thinking and feeling.

3. When you first open your eyes, look in the mirror, and notice your facial expression. Write down your impressions of your expression, noting your eyes, mouth and angle of your head.

4. List all the feelings you experience as you look at yourself, and those from your recall of the situation. Check all that seem to be reflected by your facial expression.

5. Next, turn the tape recorder on, try to get back in to the flow of the recalled situation, and speak aloud the words you remember saying at that time.

6. Play back the recording and list the impression(s) you have about how your voice sounds, such as hesitant, tentative, assured, strong, and the like.

7. Review what you wrote for steps 4 and 6. Now try to step back and become objective about yourself in this situation. Note particularly how your inner experiencing, such as feelings, was made apparent by your facial expression and/or voice tone. Also note the extent to which your vulnerability and openness were conveyed by these.

8. Take some time to think about the following, and then list what could be some possible changes for you that would make you less open, susceptible, and vulnerable.
   • What eye position and/or contact would convey more confidence in my decision?
   • How could I moderate my head position to appear less vulnerable?
   • Can I not smile, or have an open mouth position?
   • What would make my voice sound more confident and assured even if I didn't necessarily feel that way?

9. Use the mirror to practice different facial expressions, and the tape recorder to practice voice tones. Try to visualize yourself in possible situation with real people, and continue to practice these.

10. Whenever you find yourself in a similar situation again, visualize what you developed in step 9.

One final suggestion, don't explain why you are saying no. When you try to explain, you give the other person access to your feelings of guilt, shame, or inadequacy; and you provide them with information they can use to try and get you to change your mind.

FEAR OF BEING ALONE

What is referred to here is not isolation, alienation or loneliness, although all three can play a role for some people. Fear of being alone is a state where the absence of other people and activity produces intense anxiety that compels the person to seek relief. They cannot tolerate being alone as that arouses a deep and intense fear of abandonment which in turn presents the possibility that they will not survive because they are not capable of self-care.

This state is so scary that they will go to extreme measures to prevent experiencing it.

Loneliness is a temporary state, usually recognized as such by that person. He/she feels cut off from others, especially lacking meaningful interpersonal connections. Loneliness occurs for many reasons such as loss of a significant person due to death, their impaired functioning, military deployment, move to other geographical area, loss of affection, and so on. The particular person or persons are missed, and no substitute or other relationships are available.

Isolation and alienation are more severe forms of feeling cut-off. People experiencing these can feel disconnected from others in all parts of their lives, and think that they are so unacceptable that others are rejecting them, or vice versa, they are so different that they are rejecting others. They do not experience meaningful contact with others, whereas the lonely person may do so. People who feel they are isolated and/or alienated do not have meaningful contact with others.

People who fear being alone have a different situation from those experiencing loneliness or isolation and/or alienation. They can have meaningful relationships, may not feel disconnected from others, or experience other feelings associated with these states. They simply cannot become comfortable with a lack of humans in their immediate vicinity. This fear can lead to their doing some very unwise things just to not be alone. Responding positively or continuing a distressing relationship can be the result for some who take up with unsuitable lovers, especially when this happens more than once.

The anxiety that emerges can be intense and the fear of being alone very pervasive, and because these are so much a part of the person can make him/her very difficult to overcome. It can also be difficult to determine what the basic cause(s) are for such an intense, deep, and enduring reaction, and is much beyond what can be presented here. This too is a personal work that may need the assistance of a competent mental health professional. But, maybe there are some suggestions that may help in the short term.

Exercise 9.3. Being Alone

Materials: Several sheets of paper and a pen or pencil.
Procedure:

1. Find a place to work where you will not be disturbed, and have a suitable writing surface.
2. Reflect on the thoughts and the feelings you have at the moment when you think about being alone. The definition for being alone is yours, and what that means for you.
3. Review the list and add additional thoughts and feelings. You may even want to recall a particular experience that still carries thoughts and feelings you can access today.
4. Label each thought and feeling as positive (+) or negative (−), and give the thought or feeling that seems especially important or intense a double label, such as (−−).

5. Next, take each thought and feeling that has a positive label and write a description of what your body, mind and spirit experience when you have that thought or feeling. Be as descriptive as possible and try to describe as many details as you can.
6. Repeat step 5 for thoughts and feelings with negative labels.
7. Return to your list of labeled thoughts and feelings, and give each a rating for logic using the scale 0 (very illogical) to 10 (extremely logical). The determination of logical rests on your evaluation of the threat or severity of the situation that produced the thought or feeling. For example, if a thought was that no one would ever like you if this person does not care for you and it has an intense label of double negative, then the rating for logic may be 2, indicating very little logic for that thought.
8. Review your rated list and make a new list of the thoughts and feelings that have ratings of 0–5. You can title this list, Illogical Thoughts and Feelings.
9. Take each item on the new list and write a rebuttal to it that is a more realistic and logical reaction. For example, in the example given in step 7, a more realistic and logical reaction could be, "I have the capacity to be liked by others, I am liked by some, I can form new relationships where I am liked, and I am not limited to this particular one."
10. Read the list you generated for step 9, and try to really accept the validity of what you wrote. Read this several times to more firmly fix these in your mind, keep this final list, read it weekly or monthly, and/or write the items on an index card and carry it with you to read often. Remind yourself of these rebuttals to illogical thoughts and feelings whenever they arise.

Another strategy that may help combat the fear of being alone is to develop, learn, or create activities that you can do when you are alone, that capture your interest and involvement, and that produce positive feelings for you. Decide what you enjoy doing, can do alone, and then rehearse or practice these. Here are some suggestions to get you started:

- Playing a musical instrument
- Painting or sculpting
- Construct collages such as for a scrapbook
- Write anything such as poetry, stories, journal entries
- Find interesting recipes and try them out
- Read about anything that interests you
- Learn a new skill such as knot tying
- Make something in the workshop
- Go for a walk and look at everything, find new plants, hear new sounds
- Meditate for 5 minutes each day for a month and then increase the time for this by 1 minute each day until you reach 20 minutes at least. You can do more if you like.

The final strategy is to learn relaxation techniques that you can use when you become aware that you are anxious.

NEED FOR PARENTAL APPROVAL

Part of your susceptibility to unsuitable lovers may be due to your deep and enduring yearning and longing for parental love and approval. This need may have always been with you and is so much a part of you that you don't even think about it anymore, or are only dimly aware of it. This can be true even if you think that you have resolved the issue, and given up hoping for it. It can lurk in your unconscious, and influence your thoughts, behavior, and feelings in ways that are not obvious or apparent to you. Some possible indicators that you are, still as an adult, longing and yearning for parental love and approval follow:

- Hypersensitivity to perceived criticism and blame
- Oversensitivity to others' comments, that is, you tend to take these personally
- Defiance about perceived demands, orders, and the like
- Excessive need for others' liking and approval to the extent that you do things you do not want to do, or are not in your best interests
- Cannot be satisfied with what you have or do
- Overachieving
- Unrealistic and lofty aspirations and intents
- Deeply wounded by others' comments that seem devaluing of you
- Constantly tense, anxious, and panic easily
- Overresponsibility for others' welfare

You are trying hard to get this need met, and you may sometimes try to get it in ways that are not constructive for you, or from people who sense this need and exploit it for their benefit.

The other part is that you are still trying to get something that, most likely, will not be forthcoming. The parent whose love and approval you are seeking is unlikely to have an about-face and recognize his/her failure, and then atone for what was missing all these years. It would be wonderful if there was something that would get through to him/her, and there may be. However, it is futile to continue to expect a turnaround from the parent where you start getting what was lacking.

The reasons for this parental failure are not about you, it's about them and their inability to empathize, to assume a nurturing parental role, and to become less self-absorbed and focused only on their needs, concerns, and the like. But, what you are likely to have internalized from the parent's behavior and attitudes is that you are inadequate and flawed or else they would love and approve of you. You then continue to act on these misinterpreted messages received from the parent's behavior and attitudes, and also continue to try and get from others what you did not get from the parent. This can contribute to your propensity for selecting unsuitable lovers.

How could you go about changing this yearning and longing that is so deep-seated and an integral part of you? Not easily done as you probably have had this self-perception and longing for most or all of your life. This too is the kind of work that can be assisted by a competent mental health professional, and is beyond what can be presented here. There are a few suggestions that may be helpful.

Exercise 9.4. Parental Approval Longing

Procedure:

1. Become aware of how strong your longing and yearning is for parental love and approval that is not forthcoming. Try giving it a rating from 0 (very weak or nonexistent) to 10 (extremely strong).
2. Rate the realism of the thought or wish for the parent to change using the parameters in step 1.
3. Reflect on the times you've tried to convey to your parent the impact of his/her attitudes and behavior on you, and were successful at getting him/her to understand.
4. Assess the number of changes the parent made in attitude and/or behavior that seemed positive for what you requested or needed.
5. If you have a rating of 6 or more for step 1; a rating of 5 or less for step 2; a success number of 3 or less for step 3; and a change number of 2 or less for step 4, you will want to consider the possibility that your fantasy about your parent doesn't coincide with reality.

Suggestions:

1. Give up the fantasy.
2. Accept your parent as he/she is, and that he/she is unlikely to change.
3. Reflect on what and how you love and approve of yourself. Make a list of these and review them weekly.
4. Give yourself permission to feel pleased about things you do that reflect self-approval.
5. Imagine you hugging and loving your self, especially when you feel lost, adrift, confused, hurt and so on.

YOUR EMOTIONAL TRIGGERS

Manipulative and exploitive people know how to use others' emotional triggers to get what they want. The various types of unsuitable lovers can be especially adept at this because they can consciously and unconsciously tune in to these for others, and because others can lack awareness about their personal emotional triggers, and/or fail to adequately insulate themselves from having them triggered. You get hooked and played like a fisherman does to a fish. The goal is to not get hooked, although this may be a difficult task.

Let's take a look at some possible emotional triggers for each type of unsuitable lovers, and you decide which, if any, best fit you.

Type	Your Emotional Triggers
Hurting and Needy	Sympathy, pain that needs soothing, power to fix it
Risk-taking and Rebellious	Excitement, energizing, dissatisfaction with current status
Charming and Manipulative	Longing and yearning, approval and liking possibilities
Self-absorbed	Desire to connect, romance with blinders, fulfills a need
Exotic and Different	Revenge, curiosity, attention, needs, restlessness

These are just a few of possible emotional triggers, and some are very complex and cannot be adequately stated in a few words. However, you will find it very helpful to become more aware of your emotional triggers so as to better resist the lures of unsuitable lovers, and this can be difficult to do.

Further, there are some conditions and situations that can increase your susceptibility and leave you more vulnerable to have your emotions triggered such as the following:

- Experiencing personal hurt such as rejection or betrayal
- Feeling helpless to change a distressing situation in your life
- Being under the influence of drugs or alcohol; even a little can impact your insulation and boundaries
- Illness, or a temporary physical condition
- Feeling depressed, blue, down, or adrift
- Awareness of dissatisfaction in your life with no clear direction
- Aimless, lack of goals, unrealistic expectations
- Anger, fear, or other intense emotions

When you are experiencing any of these, and especially when you have two or more of them at the same time, you can be more vulnerable and emotionally susceptible. Your usual defenses are down or weaker than usual, and the person who reads this can use the opportunity to trigger your emotions with little or no resistance from you.

Recognizing when you are in a susceptible state can help you take steps that can reduce or eliminate having your emotional triggers activated. It becomes easier to resist and say no when you can tell yourself that it isn't wise to make decisions like this when you are not 100 percent. You can say to yourself that you need to wait until you are better or ready to think this through before acting on it.

Learning the event, place, or situation can also give you time to reflect on whether or not this immediate feeling is being manipulated by someone, or is a response to something within you that needs consideration because it can lead you astray, or if there are better ways to address your feelings. Time out to reflect is always helpful.

Developing and learning to use your emotional insulation is another strategy. Use the visualization of some barriers between you and the person who is trying to attract you via your emotional triggers, or when you feel the pull of the lure. This gives you some time to think about what you want, and if this relationship will be beneficial for you.

10

INCREASE YOUR INTERPERSONAL EFFECTIVENESS

Your attraction to dead-end lovers can also signal some need to increase your interpersonal effectiveness so that more suitable lovers will find you of interest, as you will find them. In this chapter we will present some information that will help to increase your self-confidence, self-esteem, and self-efficacy. The topics discussed are the following:

- Nonverbal signals
- Listening strategies
- Responding strategies
- How to see and reduce your self-absorbed behaviors and attitudes
- Feelings, how to express and manage these effectively
- Effective conflict behavior

The information and strategies are designed to help you analyze your interpersonal effectiveness so as to target changes that will help get you to become the person you envision and want to become.

NONVERBAL COMMUNICATION

Your nonverbal communication is the most important part of the signals you send to others about your self-confidence, self-esteem, current mood and feelings, your status and power, personal boundary space, and relationship to the other person(s). Most of this is unconscious on your part, but can be read and responded to in spite of your conscious perceptions and thoughts about how you are feeling and coming across to others. Let's examine some characteristics of nonverbal communication. Johnson (2003) provides ten characteristics for nonverbal communication.

- It is pervasive, always present when observing or being observed.
- You will always communicate nonverbally, it is inevitable.

- Interpretation of nonverbal communication is cultural bound, and differs among cultures.
- It is relationship oriented in that it conveys affinity, control, respect, and/or dominance.
- Nonverbal communication reveals unconscious feelings and attitudes that are sometimes at variance with the spoken words. In these cases, the nonverbal communication is generally the more truthful and accurate message.
- Its functions are to support, enhance, or contradict verbal statements.
- It is ambiguous in that the gestures and other features can have several meanings. For example, crying can be from frustration, pain, relief, or joy.
- Nonverbal messages use multiple channels, are continuous, and are primarily unconscious.
- Your nonverbal communication manages the identity you convey to others, such as friendliness, suspicion, susceptible, and so on.
- Your perception of your power and status is revealed through your nonverbal communication.

You are always communicating even when you are not speaking. Some unsuitable lovers are very adept at reading these messages, and use this information to manipulate you without you being aware of what they are doing. Let's take a look at some of the things that comprise nonverbal messages.

We'll first describe these, and then present some strategies that will help you better convey your conscious perception of your self.

Nonverbal Signals

When someone receives a nonverbal communication, it comes as a cluster of signals and is not judged by just one signal such as a gesture. Keep this in mind as you read what follows, and don't focus on just one thing as a basis for your judgment. I'll first describe and define the signals, and then try to give you an example of putting all of this together to make an interpretation. The signals that will be discussed are:

- Gestures
- Facial expression
- Eye behavior
- Voice
- Touch
- Body orientation
- Posture
- Clothing
- Use of space and distance
- Physical appearance
- Artifacts

Gestures refer to the position and movement of hands, arms, head, and legs. To give you some idea of how important these can be, visualize someone talking to you whom you think is angry, but the person denies being angry. However, what you note is that he is shaking his head at the same time his arms are crossed over his chest, and his fists are clenched. There is a disconnect between what he is saying and the gestures he is using.

Take a moment and reflect on the gestures you use or used with an unsuitable lover. What did you do with your hands, arms, head, and legs? How much movement did you use when in his/her presence? Could you have been saying one thing, while your gestures conveyed something else? Could this be why when you said "No," it was ignored?

Facial expression is a good barometer of what you are thinking and feeling at the moment, especially about the person with whom you are interacting. You may not realize the breadth and range of messages you convey via your face. People notice your expression, and will modify their approach and response to you based on how they are reading your face. Even when you are trying hard not to show what you are feeling at the moment, such as when you are hurt, your unconscious can help produce an expression that gives you away.

Some people have learned to control their facial expression. For example, performers, poker players, law enforcement officers, and others who deal with the public on a regular basis where it is important that their face not be an accurate reflection of what they are thinking and feeling can exercise much control. Indeed, that's where the term "poker face" was derived. There are other relationships where it is important that the other person be able to read you, such as in an intimate relationship. You may want to have a friend or a family member you trust give you some feedback on how revealing your facial expression is most of the time.

Eye behavior refers to the direction and length of gazing, either at someone or in their eyes. Sustained eye gaze is thought to be indicative of truthfulness, interest in the other person, and of genuineness in the United States. In other cultures, sustained eye gaze can be seen as disrespectful, aggressive, or suspicious. So, even in the United States when you are interacting with citizens who have a different cultural background, you need to be aware that they may have very different interpretations about eye behavior. This can be especially important for interpretations about female eye behavior as sustained eye contact may be perceived incorrectly because of cultural expectations for females.

Sustained eye contact in intimate relationships usually conveys interest, caring, and concern. However, this is also a means for increasing your emotional susceptibility, as you can become more open to projections that lead to projective identifications where you take on the emotions of the other person, and are manipulated by them because you have identified with them. All of this takes place on an unconscious level and you can end up being manipulated and controlled to do things you do not want to do, or are not in your best interest. You may want to reflect on whether this was your experience with an unsuitable lover.

Voice characteristics of tone, speed, pitch, volume, and the number and length of pauses also convey messages about your internal state. For example, a rapid, loud rate of speaking usually conveys hostility while a soft, slow rate conveys warmth and interest. When there are numerous pauses, this can convey tentativeness about whether or not you feel you are definite in what you are saying. Phrasing your sentences as questions instead of statements can also send a message of tentativeness, need for approval, and/or search for reassurance. You may not be aware of these actions, but these are some signals of lack of confidence and self-esteem.

You may want to pay attention to how you are saying things for a day. Attend to how many times you ask questions instead of making statements, especially when you are not really seeking information. Try taping a conversation you have with another person and listening to yourself on the playback. You may pick up some cues about your voice and speech that are conveying something different than you wish, such as a lack of self-confidence when you think you are sound confident.

Touch is an enhancer of your verbal statements. You send a message when and how you shake hands with someone (social), how you perceive the person as a friend with a hug or clap on the back, as acts of aggression even when you consider the touches to be love taps such as shoves, and your kisses can convey affection and/or sexual interest.

Touch in an intimate relationship is expected and is a part of intimacy. Because of your openness with your partner, you are more susceptible to projections and manipulations through touches, as these arouse your tender and sexual feelings. Caresses, kisses, and sexual intimacy can convey caring, love, or they can be a means of manipulation, power, and control. Touching is a very powerful nonverbal communication.

Body orientation refers to the degree and extent to which your body is turned to or away from a person. Turning toward a person where your body is straight and in line with the other person's conveys interest. A forward lean added to this indicates considerable interest. When combined with sustained eye gaze, there is probably no mistaking the interest for the other person. On the other hand, a lack of interest or moderated interest is conveyed when your body is turned away from the other person, if only turned slightly away. When there is a backward lean, that is a definite signal of disinterest or desire to get away.

You may have started to use this nonverbal signal when you were in the disillusion stage where your lover was not meeting your expectations as he/she had previously done. Or, you may have noticed his/her slightly turning away body position, and/or lack of forward lean, and correctly interpreted this as losing interest in you without conscious awareness of what triggered this thought or feeling. It could also be that, when you asked him/her if interest was lagging, the response was one that suggested that you were incorrect; you could not point to any observable behavior that suggested lack of interest as your noticing was unconscious, and you were left feeling wrong for even bringing the topic up.

Posture, when standing, sitting, and walking, is a good indicator of your internal perception of your self, your current mood, or it could be a habit that still conveys a message about how you value yourself. For example, some tall people who grew quickly may have a habit of slumping to appear shorter, especially if they are very tall. Although this is a habit for them, the message conveyed is still somewhat accurate that they are uncomfortable with their height. A lot of judgments are made by others just by observing your posture walking into a room, standing, and sitting. The following exercise may provide some valuable information.

Exercise 10.1. What My Posture Conveys

1. Stand in front of a mirror in your customary position. Don't try to stand tall unless that is what you always do. As you stand there, really examine your posture and see if you are slumping, have a strong backward lean as if you were strutting along, if your pelvis area is thrust out or thrust back, and if your head is up, down, or straight ahead. Make some notes about what you observe about yourself.
2. Ask someone to take some candid pictures of you standing and sitting when you are unaware that your picture is being taken. Look at these photographs and see what interpretations of your posture you would make if you were looking at this person.
3. Make a list of the feelings you remember experiencing at the time the pictures were taken, and judge the accuracy of matching these to your posture in the pictures.

You may find that you are nonverbally communicating more about your self than you realize, and that your posture is a good indicator of what you think of your self, and what you feel at the time.

Clothing conveys considerable information about you, or it is a signal by which others make significant judgments about you. Judgments are made about our economic level, educational level, social position, trustworthiness, sophistication, level of success, and moral character. You may not have thought that all of these could be discerned from your clothing, but it can be. For example, did you know that a majority of Americans think that a man wearing a bow tie is untrustworthy? Where that idea comes from I don't know, but it is reported in books on how to dress for success.

Are you dressing to attract the kind of lover you want? Or, are you caught up in the media presentations about having to dress provocatively to attract, and then be disappointed in the kind of person you attract? This applies to both men and women. Look at your customary clothes, and ask yourself what messages do they convey? You could be surprised at the answers you get.

Your use of space and distance unconsciously sets your personal boundaries. For example, if you unconsciously step back when you feel someone invades your personal space, especially if the person is not invited, not welcome, or not known, this signals your discomfort with having your space invaded without your permission. On the other hand, if you do not step back when this happens, then you are signaling that your personal boundaries are weak and you will accept invasion. As you can see, that behavior sends a message that you are malleable, susceptible, and subject to dominance.

Reflect on how you define your personal space and distance, and if that is being constantly violated and intruded on without your consent. You may want to think about the frequency with which you feel uncomfortable around others that could be due to violations of your personal space. Also reflect on how you may be violating other's personal space without permission, and what their reactions are. All this will help you to become more sensitive to when your personal space and distance is being violated, and becoming aware of how you can prevent being uncomfortable by taking more steps to define that boundary, and to be more discriminating about who you let get physically close to you.

Physical appearance is an enormous factor in conveying nonverbal messages, and in how others interpret these messages. Not only do you have some judgments about these, others have their opinions and these may be at variance with yours. Aspects of physical appearance that comprise messages include age, gender, body shape, body size, ethnicity, and other body characteristics. Think about it, you and others have some definite ideas and impressions about physical appearances that are appealing to you such as hair, its color, texture, and style; eyes, their color, size, and shape; height, weight, and distribution of weight; skin, its texture and color, and so on.

Try the following exercise to get a better notion of the physical appearance that appeals to you.

Exercise 10.2. Appealing Physical Attributes

Materials: Several sheets of paper and a pen or pencil.

1. Find a place to work where you will not be disturbed. Think about one former lover and either look at a photograph, or try to visualize him/her.
2. Make a list of the physical attributes that were appealing to you, such as eye color, hair texture, height, and so on.
3. Make a list of the physical attributes that person had that you did not like, or that were neutral.
4. Bring another lover to remember and visualize. Repeat steps 2 and 3 for this person. Repeat this as many times as you like.
5. Look at your lists, and write a summary about the physical attributes that are common among the lovers, especially those that are appealing to you.
6. Reflect on the possibility that you continue to be attracted to dead-end lovers because you are too focused on their physical appearance, and may be ignoring someone more suitable in more important ways because they don't meet your image for the desired physical appearance.

Let's turn to examining your physical appearance and what it conveys to others. The following list of questions can be used to focus your self-examination:

- How comfortable am I with my physical appearance at this moment?
- Am I trying to convey that I am different than I really am? For example, am I trying to appear younger, older, more contemporary, less educated, and so on than what is true for me?
- What is my social and economic status, and is this portrayed in my physical appearance? How, or how not?
- What do I want my physical appearance to say about who I am as a person, and will this attract the kind of lover that I am seeking?

Artifacts refer to jewelry and other adornments. Some people use these to serve as indicators of something important about them, such as their religious beliefs. Some people use these to show off and highlight their wealth, or at least send a message to get others to think they are wealthy, such as wearing a very expensive watch. What adornments do you look for on people you are attracted to? What judgments or conclusions do you make about others based solely or in part on their artifacts?

Scent can also be listed under artifacts when perfumes and other such scents are used by the person. I'm allergic to scent, so I have to avoid people wearing perfume, aftershave, and any strong scent. That's unfortunate because I lose the opportunity to get to know them in other ways. But, you may be making unconscious judgments about people because of the scent they are wearing. This can be true when they are wearing a scent you like, you identify as being expensive, or one that you do not like. We all use a variety of nonverbal cues to form unconscious judgments.

This brings us to considering what artifacts appeal to you, do not appeal to you, and/or those you wear to be attractive. Think about what someone would wear as an adornment that would be a turn-off for you, cause you to feel that you don't want to get to know this person, or a more neutral response such as disinterest. What adornments capture your interest, and cause you to want to know more about that person? What artifacts do you wear to try to attract the kind of person you want to get to know, and does this work? Do you need to give more thought to your adornments and the kind of messages they may be sending? Now that we've described and defined some nonverbal signals, and provided some suggestions that you can consider, let's turn to presenting some ways you can monitor your nonverbal behavior to be more reflective of the person you are, and the person you want to convey to others.

YOUR NONVERBAL SIGNALS

Our task here is to assess your nonverbal signals for the degree and extent to which you send messages about your self-confidence and self-esteem. These are the judgments made about you by others, and are signals for your openness to manipulation, emotional susceptibility, and strength of your psychological boundaries. Let's begin with this exercise.

Exercise 10.3. Assessing My Nonverbal Signals

Materials: Several sheets of paper and a pen or pencil.

1. Reproduce the following chart and fill it in. It is probably too small on this page for you to write what you want to in the space provided. However, that is also an option.
2. Write your current behavior for each signal in the space. Examples are given for possible behavior.
3. Then rate your self-confidence and self-esteem for each signal using the following scale. Rate each for how you feel you are first, and then rate how your behavior may be perceived by others.

5: High; 4: Moderate; 3: Varies, but mostly medium; 2: Varies, but mostly low; 1: Low

Nonverbal signal	Current Behavior	Self-confidence	Self-esteem	How I Feel What I Convey	How I Feel What Others Convey
Voice tone (e.g., soft, hard, tentative, etc.)	_____	_____	_____	_____	_____
Facial expression (e.g., smiles, frown, neutral)	_____	_____	_____	_____	_____
Posture (e.g., tense, relaxed, slumping, straight)	_____	_____	_____	_____	_____
Eye contact (e.g., sustained, jumpy, avoidant)	_____	_____	_____	_____	_____
Touch (e.g., accepting, avoidant, touch others)	_____	_____	_____	_____	_____
Gestures (e.g., open, constricted, exuberant, defensive)	_____	_____	_____	_____	_____
Spatial (e.g., strong personal boundaries, weak, or spongy boundaries)	_____	_____	_____	_____	_____

Scoring: Review all the ratings, and make a list of those that are rated 3 or below for how you feel and what you convey. These are the nonverbal signals that you may want to target for change, especially if these are signaling that you are susceptible, or that your defenses are so strong that you are unapproachable.

Your nonverbal behavior is communicating your inner state, and this can be the long-term task for you, that of changing your self-perception, self-confidence, and self-esteem. If these are overinflated you will need to make them more realistic, and if they are underinflated you need to build them. The exercises in the last three chapters can get you started on this journey. Working with a competent mental health professional can help accelerate the process. Let's move to other strategies for increasing your interpersonal effectiveness; understanding the elements of effective communication, listening and responding; and ineffective communication, listening and responding.

EFFECTIVE AND INEFFECTIVE COMMUNICATION

Effective communications have the following characteristics:

- It is two-way
- Both content and feelings are heard and understood
- The vocabulary used by the speaker is appropriate for the receiver
- All means are used to ensure that the communication is clear and unambiguous

Two-way communication recognizes the importance for both the speaker and the receiver. The speaker needs to feel that his/her communication was heard and understood, and the receiver needs to have the ability to hear the spoken words and understand the speaker's meaning. Included in the two-way communication are *content and feelings*. The receiver hears the content and the underlying feelings embedded in the content. Many times the feelings are more important than the words used. The *vocabulary* used by either the speaker or the receiver is appropriate and assumptions are not made about understanding of concepts, jargon, and unusual words. It is very frustrating to both when the communication has to be interrupted to explain these. Effective communication is clear and unambiguous, but there are things that often get in the way of obtaining this clarity. For example, people under the influence of emotional intensity, medication, self-absorption, irrational logic, and the like are often not clear in their speaking, or focused enough in their receiving to be clear and unambiguous. There are cultural, diversity, regional, and gender differences that can also be factors to prevent clear and unambiguous communication.

Ineffective communications are actions like the following:

- Giving orders
- Using or implying should and ought
- Suggesting that you know or have all the answers

- Inferring motives and reasons for the other person
- Ignoring the person's problems and concerns
- Rushing to rescue the other person to prevent your feeling his/her emotional intensity
- Using a barrage of questions as a way to show interest
- Ignoring the person's emotional intensity
- Generalizing, such as using the words always and never
- Calling the person names or labeling him/her

Make a note of these ineffective communication behaviors, and monitor your interactions to determine if or how often you use these.

LISTENING AND RESPONDING

This strategy has two goals: to help you learn to listen for meaning, feeling, and content, and to provide you with responses to convey what you heard and understood. You need to be aware that these strategies can backfire in that they show interest in the other person, can lead you to be more emotionally susceptible, but they also increase your effectiveness in relating to others, and this alone could bring more "winners" into your life. At the very least, the strategies will increase the quality of your other relationships. We'll tackle listening first.

Listening involves having an emotional presence, screening out distractions, ceasing talking, and focusing on the speaker. In other words, your attention is on the speaker to the exclusion of other people, yourself, and environmental events at the time. This is not as easy to do as it sounds.

Reflect on your last conversation with anyone and recall if you did any of the following:

- Look around the room
- Mentally formulate your response
- Interrupt the speaker
- Think about your concerns, what you need to do, and the like
- Look at someone or something other than the speaker
- Move a lot, have nervous gestures, fiddle with your hair, coins in your pocket, and so on

These are all actions that can signal disinterest, and take your attention away from the speaker and what he/she is saying and meaning. You lose some valuable information when you don't fully listen. On the other hand, these are actions to use when you are not interested, want to reduce your openness to projections, and want to decrease your emotional susceptibility.

To become a more effective listener you will want to practice focusing on the speaker, hearing the words, trying to discern the feelings the speaker has at the moment, and refrain from thinking about your concerns, formulating a response to the speaker, or looking away from the speaker. You simply are there to take in everything that person wants to communicate. Practice doing this the next time you talk to anyone, and notice the results. Practice with family and friends as much as possible, remind yourself to listen when you find that you are doing any of the actions above, and become aware of how much you are not really listening to the other person, you are focused on your concerns or distracted by something else.

Effective responding has two stages; the first is to ensure that you are accurate in your understanding of what the speaker meant, and the second is to tap into the feelings around the communication and acknowledge these. Responding is not any of the following:

- Giving advice
- Telling someone what they should or ought to do
- Recounting a personal story about a similar experience
- Minimizing the speaker's feelings as irrational or illogical, even if this could be the case
- Changing the topic to get away from the emotional intensity
- Ignoring the speaker's feelings
- Focusing only on the content
- Blaming or criticizing
- Inappropriate questioning

A skill that you can develop to help you respond more effectively is called paraphrasing. This is the first phase and simply ensures that what you heard was what the person said, and/or gives the speaker an opportunity to check out if he/she said what he/she meant to say. Paraphrasing involves the following:

- Restating of the content using different words
- The intent of the message is not changed
- The paraphrasing doesn't elaborate on the message
- Paraphrasing is not parroting what the speaker said
- Questions are not paraphrasing

When you paraphrase, you simply repeat the content using different words. For example, let's suppose you are talking to a friend who tells you that he is struggling with a decision. Which of the following would be a paraphrase?

1. What can I do to help you?
2. What do you need to make a decision about?
3. Don't you just hate it when you have to make a decision, and you can't think of what to do?
4. You have a decision to make and you are trying to sort through your options.

While all the answers are common ones that people make, only number 4 is a paraphrase. Let's try an exercise on paraphrasing to give you some practice.

Exercise 10.4. Paraphrasing

Materials: A sheet of paper and a pen or pencil.
Procedure: Read each of the following statements, and write a paraphrase. Suggested paraphrases are at the end of the chapter.

1. *I'm really discouraged. Everything is going wrong in my life, and I don't know how to fix it.*
2. *My job is driving me crazy.*
3. *My sister is being really mean to me.*
4. *I really need to pass this class.*

The other part of effective communication is appropriate responding. You first have to listen intently and when you respond, pay attention to the following:

- Your openness to hearing what the person has to say.
- Stop talking.
- Become less self-absorbed.
- Listen for spoken and unspoken feelings.
- Don't formulate your response while the other person is talking. Try to stay in the moment, focused on him/her.
- Don't use your response to promote solutions, to "fix" it, to give advice, and other such responses.

Openness may not always be easy to have as you may have some reactions to the person, a particular opinion about the relationship, or have your own set of concerns. All of these can interfere with your capacity at the moment to be open to really hearing the other person. It goes without saying that you cannot listen if you are talking. But, I've found that there are numerous people who don't stop talking when others are trying to talk to them, so this can be important to say. *Stop talking,* attend to the speaker, and bring your cognitive and emotional self to the conversation. *Become less self-absorbed* means to stay aware that every conversation does not have you as the center. Indices of self-absorption are lack of empathy, changing the topic to something about you, deflecting the speaker's feelings so that you don't have to cope with them, focusing more on your feelings than on their feelings, and having the answer(s) for them. *Listening for spoken and unspoken feelings* will be a major source of information for making appropriate responses that show your understanding of what the other person is experiencing. You'll want to check out the accuracy of what you think or sense the speaker is feeling, and that's presented in the next section. While it is tempting, or may be your habit, it is best to *not try to formulate your response* while the other person is talking. When you are thinking about what you want to say, you are not entirely focused on the other person. First, make a paraphrasing response, and this will give you the time you need to think about the rest of your response. You can think a lot faster than you can talk, and this gap provides you with an ample opportunity to think. You may want to provide solutions, "*fix it*," or make the problem go away, and your response is designed to do any of these. However, unless it is a crisis which requires a different kind of response, the most effective responses are those that are described in the next section.

Effective Responses

Try to use the following as a guide for making effective responses. Your responses should have the following characteristics:

- Your words should convey that you are sensing the speaker's inner experiencing.
- You make statements instead of asking questions.
- What you say identifies and communicates the speaker's feelings out loud, and/or your feelings.
- To understand what the speaker is feeling, you may want to tune in to your inner experiencing for clues, and to try to feel what the person is feeling.

When your response notes what the other person is feeling, this conveys to him/her that you are interested in understanding him/her at a deep level, and that you care about him/her. You really don't have to do this with everyone, but there are times when even a stranger can appreciate being understood. You cannot just say that you know what the person is feeling as that may or may not be true. You have to name, label, and identify the feeling in some way, and what you say should be a feeling, not a thought about a feeling. Following is a list of some feeling words under categories for common feelings. Read these and think about how often you use these words. You know them, but are likely to use only a very few in your conversations. We'll categorize these as anger, fear, happiness, and sadness.

Anger	Fear	Happiness	Sadness
Irritation	Discomfort	Pleasure	Unhappy
Annoyance	Apprehension	Cheer	Dejected
Displeased	Dread	Delight	Depressed
Agitated	Distressed	Enjoyment	Gloomy
Furious	Trepidation	Gratified	Woeful
Rage	Terror	Joy	Grief

It could be helpful to learn some feeling words, and to practice using these in conversations.

A source of information about what the other person is feeling can be your *inner experiencing*. This is one way that your taking in of projections can be useful. You may be feeling what the other person is feeling because he/she projected the feeling and you took it in without realizing what you were doing. You will want to prevent your taking in of others' projections until your self is strong enough to resist incorporating these projections and making them a part of you. When you are strong enough you can open yourself to the projection and feel that it will be blocked from incorporation into your self as part of you. At this point, you will still feel the projected feelings, but know that it is coming from the other person. When this happens, you can use that feeling to better understand what the other person is feeling. Experienced therapists can do this so as to increase their ability to be empathic. That's why it can be important to fortify and develop your self so as to prevent taking in of projections unless you understand and accept what you are doing.

REDUCE SELF-ABSORPTION

Let's begin this presentation with an exercise to give you some idea of self-absorbed behaviors and attitudes you may not be aware that you have and exhibit.

Exercise 10.5. Assessment of Self-absorption

Materials: A sheet of paper and a pen or pencil.
Directions: Rate yourself on each item using the following scale.

1: Never or almost never
2: Seldom
3: Frequently
4: Very often
5: Always or almost always

1. I want to be the center of attention.	5 4 3 2 1
2. I need to be liked and admired by everyone or almost everyone.	5 4 3 2 1
3. I have a tendency to become enmeshed in others' emotions.	5 4 3 2 1
4. I have a tendency to become overwhelmed by others' emotions.	5 4 3 2 1
5. I feel I should be treated as unique and special.	5 4 3 2 1
6. I do or say things that make the difference for others.	5 4 3 2 1
7. I want to have others do what I want or expect them to do.	5 4 3 2 1
8. I feel that others have the secret to happiness.	5 4 3 2 1
9. I envy others their achievements, possessions, and/or relationships.	5 4 3 2 1
10. I want to associate with, and be associated with people of higher status such as those who are talented, rich, well-known and the like.	5 4 3 2 1

After rating yourself, you may want to get someone you trust to rate their perceptions of you on these items. Be aware that they are likely to be reluctant to do so, fearful of offending you, but if you can get beyond this, you could get some valuable information about behaviors and attitudes that you simply cannot see in yourself.

Scoring:

41–50: Considerable self-absorbed behaviors and attitudes
31–40: Numerous self-absorbed behaviors and attitudes
21–39: Some self-absorbed behaviors and attitudes
11–20: Few self-absorbed behaviors and attitudes
0–10: Little or no self-absorbed behaviors and attitudes

Reducing your self-absorbed behaviors and attitudes involve several steps:

1. Increase awareness
2. Monitor behavior
3. Explore attitudes and their behavioral manifestations for needed attention
4. Target one or two behaviors to try to change, monitor these, and when the change seems to have taken hold, target additional behaviors

---

First, you have to become aware of what you are doing and saying that are reflective of self-absorption. Just as the self-absorbed dead-end lover cannot see his/her troubling behaviors, so too are you not able to see yours. When others try to make you aware of the impact of these behaviors and attitudes on them, you can easily explain, rationalize, or deny their existence just as some dead-end lovers do. What can be helpful is for you to allow yourself to entertain the idea that you do have some behaviors and attitudes that are self-absorbed, and that you want to change these. Once you become more open to the possibility, you can begin to monitor yourself to determine what behaviors and attitudes you want to change.

Monitoring your behaviors and attitudes requires you to notice what you are doing, saying, feeling, and thinking most of the time. You also need to have a list of some specific behaviors that reflect the self-absorption such as what are you doing that is reflective of attention seeking one of the signals for possible self-absorption. An abbreviated list of some examples of behaviors for self-absorption is at the end of this chapter. A couple of books that can be helpful to learn about such behaviors are *Coping with Infuriating, Mean, Critical People* (Brown, 2006) and *Working with the Self-Absorbed* (Brown, 2003).

Exploring attitudes can be a little more difficult to do as these are internal and unique to the person, and are inferences gleamed from certain behaviors. You will want to explore the possibility that you may have some of the following attitudes:

- Grandiosity—all knowing, all seeing, all wise
- Entitlement—deserving of special and preferential attention
- Unique and special—a cut above everyone else and should be deferred to by others
- Extensions of self—others exist to serve you, are under your control, and should do what you tell them to do
- Want to be envied and admired

Target one or two behaviors that you want to change, or that you think could be improved and develop an action plan for the change(s). Trying to make too many changes all at once will become frustrating and overwhelming, which leads to giving up. If you limit yourself to one or two behavioral changes, you are more likely to see how it can be done, to be motivated to stick with it, and the feedback you receive will be reinforcing. Change takes time, but is worth the effort.

Behavioral Signs of Self-Absorption

1. Attention-seeking

   Speaks loudly, often and at length
   Interrupts others who are speaking
   Makes "grand" entrances and exits
   Sulks
   Goes from table to table in a restaurant
   Conversations are usually about the person him/herself

2. Admiration-seeking

   Nominates self for awards and recognitions
   Devalues others
   Boasts and brags
   Takes unearned credit for other's work
   Always expects gratitude and recognition

3. Grandiosity

   Inflates accomplishments
   Accepts more tasks than is reasonable to accomplish
   Oversensitive to perceived criticism
   Feels superior to others
   Arrogant, contemptuous
   Demands deference from others

4. Extensions of self

   Gives orders and expects to be promptly obeyed
   Demands/expects favors, but does not reciprocate
   Uses others' possessions without permission
   Does not knock on doors, or wait for an invitation to enter someone's space

5. Entitlement

   Pushes to the head of the line
   Expects preferential treatment
   Lies, cheats, distorts, and misleads
   Manipulates others for personal gain
   Ignores rules and regulations or laws

6. Shallow emotions

   Openly expresses few emotions
   Ignores others' feelings

Uses the correct words, but does not experience the feeling
Does not feel many emotions

7. Lack of empathy

Tells others to not overreact, be illogical, etc.
Minimizes others' feelings
Changes the topic when others are trying to express their feelings

Suggested paraphrases

1. You're concerned that your life is not as you want it to be, and you don't know how to change that.
2. Things are happening at your job that you don't understand.
3. Your sister is doing and saying things that you find offensive.
4. You're concerned about your grade in this class.

11

BECOME A WINNER AND CHOOSE WINNERS

You've probably got the idea that the real work is done with you to give you the resources to stop picking unsuitable lovers, and most of the suggestions and strategies presented in prior chapters have focused on this. The present and last chapter moves to a different level to discuss choosing suitable lovers. Chapter 1 described a mutually satisfying healthy intimate relationship, and this chapter describes how to recognize suitable lovers, and how you can check yourself to make better choices and not be under the influence of your lures.

USE STAADA

Let's start this chapter off with a simple set of thoughts and behaviors you can use that can give you the time you may need to reflect on the suitability of the person, the positives or negatives for the potential relationship, and if you are in a state where you can make informed decisions. See the previous chapter for examples of states where your informed decision-making abilities may be temporarily impaired, and it would be in your best interest to delay making decisions, especially any that are so important to the integrity of your self. The acronym for this reflective set of thoughts and behaviors is STAADA.

S—Stop, hold, desist, time out
T—Think before you act
A—Analyze your reactions
A—Affirm your self-worth, will, and determination
D—Delay acting on the attraction
A—Attend to what he/she does and not what he/she says

Stop

Mentally take time out to reflect on how you feel, what's attracting you and are you able to make your best decisions at this moment. Reflecting will not take long, can be done at anytime, and will let you focus on your experiencing.

This is a time when you can listen to your inner guide, gut-level reactions that would not usually be heard because you may attend more to the feelings generated by the attraction such as lust or yearning for a connection, or allow your thinking to be in charge of you rather than your impulses. Stopping can be especially helpful when you are under the influence of even one drink, emotionally vulnerable because of life circumstances, or just feeling down for a variety of reasons. It doesn't take long to take a mental break, and it does give you time to reflect on what you are starting to do and feel.

Whatever happened to spontaneity? Shouldn't that be a part of the connection? Doesn't that make it more exciting? If you have been attracted to several, more than two, unsuitable lovers, then it is likely that your spontaneity is more impulsive, you make unwise choices and decisions, and the excitement generated has led you to do things that are not in your best interests. Any one of these is a sufficient reason to try another way to react to a potential lover. Further, when you understand yourself better, and build undeveloped parts of self, then you will find it easier and more acceptable to stop.

Think

Think before you act is an old adage that still has some wisdom. If you are the sort of person who tends to react or act on the basis of your feelings, then you can get caught up in these and become more emotionally susceptible under certain conditions, and this can give you more vulnerability to the enticements of unsuitable lovers. Your psychological boundary strength can be a factor in your acting on your feelings, especially when the act would tap into or relieve those that are a part of what lures you to unsuitable lovers.

Some thought questions you can ask yourself are the following:

- What's attracting me right now?
- What is he/she doing or saying that I find appealing?
- What is most noticeable about this person?
- What is my first impression of him/her?
- What characteristics does he/she have that are similar to mine? Dissimilar?

Let's take one hypothetical example and run through the questions. Suppose you are attracted to the hurting and needy type, your answers could be similar to the following attraction for you—he/she looks like he/she could use some cheering up.

- What's the appeal—no smile, depressed posture, needs a hug.
- Most noticeable—the air of vulnerability, seems lost and adrift, not confident.
- First impression—he/she needs someone to care for him/her.
- Similar characteristic—"wears feelings on sleeve," facial expression reveals feelings.
- Different characteristic—seems less able to care for him/herself than I am.

Even reading this example doesn't take long, and you can think even faster.

Analyze

Use more thoughts to analyze your reactions to this person. The answers to "think" can lead to further questions and more answers. You'll need to ask yourself some "why" questions in the analysis, associate this experiencing with previous ones, and explore what it is you are looking for and if this person has the potential or cares enough to provide it. Questions such as the following can be a guide:

- Am I attracted because my lures got activated?
- Could it be that I am projecting on to that person my needs, such as needing a hug, and then reacting to him/her on my need?
- I'm drawn to this person, but don't really know what he/she is really like. Am I reacting on the basis of my first impressions?
- Has something like this happen to me before?
- Was this outcome positive or negative?
- What am I looking for or what do I want right now, and is this realistic, or in my best interest?
- Am I in a vulnerable state and too emotionally susceptible?
- Am I too open and trusting? Are my boundaries sufficiently strong at this moment?

Once you get this far, you may already have initiated some caution. You will want to be cautious and tentative if you are under the influence even if this is mild, on the rebound, feeling lost or vulnerable, angry because of relationship problems, depressed, have a physical illness such as a cold, or have any other condition that leaves you less than 100 percent. Find other ways to support and/or distract yourself. You'll make better relationship choices if you do some analyzing about the attraction.

Affirm

It can be extremely important to affirm your self-worth before initiating contact, or entering a relationship. Remind yourself of the following:

- Your value and worth as a unique person
- Your strengths and positive qualities
- That you do some things well or very well
- The meaning and purpose you have for your life, or are developing
- You are cherished and loved, or have been, or can be again

You may also have some other self-affirmations that could be of assistance. These affirmations remind you of your positive qualities, and that you value yourself as worthwhile. This is a necessary condition for others to value you, as they tend to accept your self-valuation even when this is nonconscious on your part.

Some unsuitable lovers can quickly pick up on your perception of how you feel about your self from your nonverbal behavior. If your posture, facial expression, and other nonverbal cues point to a deflated perception of self, they can take advantage of this as you are likely to be open and vulnerable to their enticements and manipulation. They can read your self-perception and level of self-esteem in many ways, but your nonverbal communication is a prime source for this information. Categories of nonverbal cues that signal susceptibility can include the following:

- Posture, and gait when moving
- Facial expression
- Clothing choice(s)
- Head position
- Eye contact
- Position and use of arms, hands, legs
- Extent of forward lean when interacting
- Allow violations of your personal space
- Acceptance of uninvited touching
- Voice tone and speech pattern

Your inner self is less hidden than you may think, and affirming yourself could make a difference both within you, and for the self that others will see.

If you have chosen several unsuitable lovers (two or more), you will also want to use this period to reaffirm your will and determination to make better choices. Tell yourself that you've made some changes that will help, no matter how modest these changes may be; that you better understand yourself and your lures; and that you don't have to continue making mistakes about relationships. You are not helpless or hopeless, you can and will do better.

Delay

Please consider the positive aspects for delaying acting on the attraction until you have more information about this person's suitability or unsuitability for you. You aren't telling him/her everything about you, and you should expect the same in return. Delay can be extremely important when you are thinking about, contemplating, or are becoming catapulted into an intimate relationship. If the other person is worth entering into this kind of relationship, he/she is worth taking some time to get to know as a person.

Romantic blinders can promote impulsive behavior and impaired judgment, so you do want to take this into consideration. Even under these circumstances when you are feeling the strong attraction, it seems to be mutual, you both are enjoying each other's company, the sexual energy is high, and an air of excitement surrounds you, you can stay in touch with the possibility that romance is blinding you, and make appropriate corrections for that. Just because you are feeling, something doesn't mean you must act on that feeling.

Suppose that you are impatient and/or impulsive, and the notion of delaying action on an attraction doesn't appeal, or seems foreign. You may think that you exercise enough control, know what you are doing, or it doesn't make sense to you to try and delay. You may even wonder what to do that would be a delaying tactic.

Eagerness, being excited, and having a romantic lure can combine to allow you to act on these feelings without sufficient thought. Even when you are able to think and analyze, the pull of the unsuitable lover can be so strong that you throw caution to the wind, and act on your feelings. After all, those are more pleasurable than are the thoughts, or lack of action. You want what you want, and you want it now. If you were to reflect on that last statement, you would see the similarities between it and the attitudes and behaviors of toddlers. While what they want is satisfaction of a basic need, such as food and attention, adults exhibiting this attitude and behavior are trying to satisfy more complex needs, but the attitude and behavior are the same. So, if you are more comfortable with rushing in and acting on impulse, you may want to think about how you can develop more adult responses.

Three Delaying Strategies

Three delaying strategies are distract, suppress, and substitute. *Distract* yourself and go somewhere this person is not present, and do something that engages your attention. If you keep doing this for awhile, you'll find that you can think clearer. *Suppression* of feeling is a defense mechanism that many people use to keep from being aware of these feelings. Usually unconscious in nature, you can also consciously use this mechanism as a delaying technique. Whatever way you usually use or initiate, suppression can be used to delay. *Substitution* of other thoughts, activities, and even imagining a place of peace, or a place where you are safe, can be delaying techniques.

Attend

Many signals and signs of unsuitability are present from the very beginning of these relationships, but you can be unaware of these, ignore them, or minimize these. You do this because of your attraction to the person; your unmet needs, wishes, and desires; the yearning and longing you have for meaningful connections; and your unresolved issues and unfinished business from past experiences. You may even have realized later about prior relationships that all the unsuitable signs were there, and wondered how you could have missed these. One simple reason could be that you were focused on getting your needs met to the point where your awareness was impaired, suppressed, or even denied. You saw, but you did not allow yourself to realize or accept what you were seeing. Then too, the other person was probably putting up a good front or facade, had learned to hide some negative characteristics, and was trying to make a good impression much like everyone does. So, between the two of you, one clueless, unaware, and wanting to stay that way to promote romance; and the other looking for a "mark" (a target, patsy, etc.), a relationship is formed on a weak and shifting basis.

You can help yourself to recognize unsuitable lovers by attending to what they do, not what they say or say that they do. This requires that you know what they have done, and what they are doing now. Read the list for clear signs of unsuitability provided in Chapter 3 for some of their actions that you need to attend to and to stay aware of their implications of these for their relationships. But, even from the first conversation, there can be some verbal signs that may suggest possible caution on your part.

- Bragging and boasting can signal significant attention and admiration needs, and a superiority attitude.
- Engaging in one-upmanship signals strong competitive behavior, needs, and the like.
- Devaluing, deriding, and other negative comments about others can signal a need to be superior, lack of empathy, and a lack of respect or tolerance for differences.
- Whining, carping, and complaining either constantly or about numerous things or people can signal needs for power, control, and to be superior.
- Collecting personal affronts, hurts, and offenses can signal a lack of personal responsibility, a desire for revenge or comeuppance, and feeling victimized.
- Blaming others for his/her troubles or misfortunes, especially when there are numerous ones, or very serious ones, can signal a lack of personal responsibility.
- Tales of putting one over on others, fooling them, and/or besting them using questionable acts can signal lying, cheating, and manipulation.
- Withhold personal information that would generally be a part of social intercourse, not personal or intrusive for most people can signal secretiveness, past illegal and other shameful activities, other significant current relationships such as marriage, lack of employment, or other signs of unsuitability.

Now that you have a tool, STAADA, to get you through the initial rush of feelings that have led to choosing unsuitable lovers in the past, we now move to presenting some ideas about recognizing suitable lovers.

You completed an exercise in Chapter 1 that you may want to review, "what am I looking for." This exercise helped you clarify the characteristics you think are important in a suitable or ideal lover. That chapter also described elements of a positive, meaningful, and satisfying relationship. The exercises completed in Chapters 2–9 give you some more information about your self and about unsuitable lovers. Putting all of this together can help you understand what you are looking for, how your needs and desires play into your choices, and how not to be misled by these to continue to select unsuitable lovers.

There are a few more ideas and suggestions that may be helpful. What signs of suitability should you look for? There are two sets that will be described. The first set, "inner resources," refers to some behaviors and attitudes that signal being centered and grounded, sufficient and appropriate boundary strength, significant completion of developmental tasks for healthy adult narcissism, and an ability to reach out and connect with others in meaningful ways. The second set of external behavior refers to his/her behavior toward you, and the feelings you have when with the person that affirms your self-worth.

YOUR WINNING SIDE—INNER RESOURCES

These are personality characteristics and developed traits that form character—who the person is that guides his/her thoughts, behaviors, attitudes and so on. These cannot be directly seen, but can be inferred by their consistent behavior. It is important to look at the characteristic behavior over time, as most everyone can act in an uncharacteristic way at times, but not consistently do so over time. Read the following list and give each a rating for its importance for a potential lover to you. Ratings are 1 (little or no importance) to 5 (extremely important).

Exercise 10.1. Important Characteristics in a Lover

1. Confident, but not arrogant or cocky
2. Able to appropriately delay gratification
3. Is not overwhelmed by life's absurdities, problems, and so on
4. Understands and respects his/her psychological boundaries and those of others
5. Has meaning and purpose for his/her life
6. Persists in spite of adversity
7. Able to demonstrate tolerance and respect for differences
8. Accepts personal responsibility for mistakes, errors, and behavior
9. Can be appropriately empathic
10. Has a secure self and set of positive values, principles, morals and ethics

---

Let's describe each of these and what your ratings may mean.

Confident, but not cocky or arrogant, describes a person with positive and strong self-esteem. The confident person knows much about his/her self and is aware and accepting of personal limitations. This person believes in his/her self-efficacy, but does not try to take on more than is realistic, possible, or reasonable. He/she thinks things through; assesses the pros, cons, and risks; and is able to judge the dangers and chances for success. A high rating for this characteristic may suggest that you had some negative experiences and/or outcomes with someone who was arrogant or cocky, and you now value the difference between these traits and cockiness.

Delaying gratification indicates some maturity as it is the immature adult who has a childish attitude and expectation that he/she is entitled to have what is wanted, and to have it immediately. Mature adults have more realistic expectations, especially when other people are involved, and they accept that if they cannot have what is wanted immediately, that it should or will be forthcoming in the future. They are not angered, frustrated, or blaming because they have to wait.

Not being overwhelmed by what life presents can get to be a challenge at times. There are so many things that impact us that are not under our control, nor do we have the power to do anything to keep them from impacting us. Examples of these are war, inflation, the economy, decisions by agencies such as social security and insurance companies. Many times you can be knocked for a loop, or have your world turned upside down by events in the community or world that you could not have predicted or prevented. It is understandable that people feel overwhelmed at times. But, when looking for a suitable lover you will want to focus on someone who does not become overwhelmed frequently, and/or had difficulty getting centered, stabilized, and grounded after these unexpected and unwelcome life events. Some personal events that can overwhelm people, and if they don't overcome these can signal possible trouble for relationships are death of a loved one with complicated mourning that persists; abandonment by a parent; physical, emotional, and/or sexual abuse; immigration and assimilation; and divorce. Some people do not move on from these traumatic events, and this is where a considerable amount of their energy goes.

Respects psychological boundaries for self and for others has a clear understanding that others are separate and distinct from him/her, and is comfortable with letting others have some private thoughts, ideas, and feelings. He/she is not threatened or anxious that others do not reveal everything, nor reveals their thoughts and feelings all of the time. He/she thinks that others have the right and power to determine the level and extent of their self-disclosures, and expects the same courtesy in return, does not push or demand disclosure, nor will he/she sulk, become angry or other commit such acts when disclosure is not forthcoming. Questions are asked for information and clarification, and phrased in a way that does not put the other person on the spot. He/she can be content with what others choose to provide and decides for himself/herself what he/she wants to provide others, and resists demands by others that feel exploitive, disrespectful, and/or intrusive.

Meaning and purpose for life is very important and affirming for each of us. There seems to be a human need that transcends all other characteristics, to live a life that has meaning and purpose. This is also one of the characteristics of people who are centered and grounded, who act in accord with their values and principles, have a zest for life, are able to persist through adversity and difficult times, maintain realistic and reasonable hope, and understand the responsibilities for love and for freedom. These people have examined and chosen their values, live by their principles, attend to others in the world, and can reexamine their meaning and purpose for life when necessary. Living a meaningful and purposeful life produces a person who has many positive and admirable characteristics.

Persistence during adverse times reflects hope, determination, a sense of self-efficacy, and can even be suggestive of loyalty and fidelity. Of course, this persistence is tempered by reality so that the energy and effort expended is not entirely futile. This kind of persistence is seen in parents who care for a disabled child, husbands and wives who ensure proper medical care when the other cannot do this for himself/herself, loss of one's job or forced retirement, unfair treatment, racism and prejudice, and so on. Persistent people do not always win, but they do try and give it their best shot. A suitable lover would have realistic persistence during adversity.

Tolerance and respect for differences indicates an understanding and the value for various perspectives, that differences among and between people are not an indication of superiority or of inferiority, and an ability to be accepting of people as they are, and not have some category or pigeonhole others must fit. This characteristic can be very positive for an intimate relationship where he/she doesn't expect or demand that you change just to become more like some preconceived notion he/she has of what is wanted in a person.

The person who is tolerant and accepting of differences does not do any of the following as examples:

- Make disparaging remarks about others' looks, body build, skin color, or other such physical characteristics
- Devalue others who are different in any way, such as having less money, being in a low or lower paid job, or from a different background or culture
- Refuse to associate with someone because of status, race, religion, and so on
- Tell jokes or stories that belittle someone focusing on a physical characteristic or disability, race or ethnic group, religion, country of origin, and the like
- Make disparaging remarks about anyone who has different interests, abilities, misfortunes
- Laugh when others are put at a disadvantage or in a lowered position about a characteristic over which they have no control, nor can change, such as height, gender, skin color, and so on

Acceptance of personal responsibility is an indication of maturity. No one likes to make mistakes, and do everything to avoid these, but these happen anyway. Most mistakes and errors are modest, but some are major and influence and/or impact others. There are even some that are devastating such as air strikes that hit the wrong target and kill people. There are times when mistakes are covered up, or don't come to anyone's attention, and can be concealed. Other times, they can be visible for everyone to see.

Personal choices and decisions have some of the same characteristics, outcomes, and implications. But, the responsible and secure person can set aside his/her reluctance to admit mistakes and so on, and accept that he/she is responsible, and not try to hide what could be perceived as a flaw.

Perceiving oneself, or the fear that others will perceive you as flawed, inadequate, shameful, and as being inferior are some feelings that fuel the refusal or reluctance to accept responsibility for mistakes, personal actions, decisions, and choices. The refusing person wants to be perceived as perfect or almost perfect, as adequate or superior, and as not shameful. Thus, they cannot and will not admit to making mistakes, nor will they accept personal responsibility for their actions, choices, or decisions.

The mature responsible person can accept personal responsibility and does not try to off-load it onto someone else, or blame extenuating circumstances all or most of the time. There are times when others and/or circumstances contribute to the mistake, action, or choices, but not always, and there can be both personal and other contributions. The unsuitable lover probably cannot tolerate a self-perception that accepts personal flaws, nor can he/she tolerate others' perception of him/her as flawed or inadequate in some way. They work hard to preserve the facade.

Appropriately empathic means that the person can be empathic with some people, some or much of the time. It is not realistic or safe to be or to try and be empathic with everyone all of the time as that is not safe. It is good enough and affirming for relationships to be appropriately empathic. Empathy is a characteristic of healthy adult narcissism where the person is self-caring and self-reflective, but is not self-absorbed and can reach out and connect with others in meaningful and enduring ways. Self-absorbed people, and those who have insufficient self development, can lack empathy and be self-absorbed. Thus, appropriate empathy is a desirable characteristic for suitable lovers.

What are some indices of empathy? I probably don't have to describe these as everyone knows what it's like to have someone empathize with them. But, here are a few clues:

- The empathic person really listens and verbally identifies what you are feeling
- Is able to put your feelings into words when you cannot
- Does not make value judgments about your feelings as being right or wrong
- Does not try to get you to stop feeling as you do
- Uses words that seem to understand the impact of your feelings
- Does not try to get you to rationalize your feelings
- Does not use deflection, distraction, or other such strategies to try and diffuse your feelings
- Does not say things that minimize your feelings

Do not be misled by phony empathic responding where the person has the words, but not the feeling. They want to appear as empathic, but either cannot access the feelings as in the case of self-absorbed people who have shallow emotions and do lack empathy, or they want you to think they are empathic so as to manipulate and exploit this for their benefit.

Suitable lovers will have all of the following *positive characteristics* to some degree, although some may need more development, and he/she is working on this.

- A secure self that is sensitive, caring, and protected, but not overly so
- A set of positive values that guide his/her thoughts, attitudes, ideas, feelings, and behavior
- Positive principles that guide his/her perceptions and treatment of others, and that form his/her character
- Moral and ethical codes that factor into his/her decisions, actions, and treatment of others

A secure self can care for and interact with others and not be easily offended, overwhelmed, take things said and done as personal attacks much of the time, be suspicious of everyone or almost everyone, go on the offense at the least sign they perceive as disrespect and other such negative acts. These secure people neither apologize for everything just when apologies are warranted, nor do they expect others to constantly apologize. His/her self is developed to the point where he/she is both self-accepting and accepting of others as worthwhile, unique, separate, and distinct.

Suitable lovers will have values that are positive and affirming of self and of others. They will value strong committed relationships as they recognize the significant contributions these make to a meaningful and purposeful life. They are not drawn to people and acts that devalue people, principles, morals and/or ethics.

Positive principles guide suitable lovers' behavior for self and for others. These principles respect the rights of others as individuals who do not only exist to serve him/her, or to be manipulated and/or exploited. They do not see cheating, lying, stealing, or violence toward others as self-affirming, and try to live their lives by their positive principles.

Moral and ethical codes are generally developed through contact with family, the community, and other sources such as school and religious institutions. These codes are taught, but some aspects are just internalized from observation and understanding of others' unconscious expectations. However learned and incorporated, the suitable lover will have some parts of their moral and ethical codes that prevent them form taking advantage of others, engaging in illegal acts constantly and/or encouraging others to do so, seducing others to do things they do not want to do that can be destructive and are not in that person's best interests, and using others for personal gain.

EXTERNAL BEHAVIOR

The previous section discussed some internal resources and characteristics for suitable lovers. These can only be known by inferences from their behavior over time. We now turn to external behavior that can signal suitability.

- Appropriately gives and receives affection
- Attends to you without being overpowering, smothering, or becoming enmeshed
- Interested in you and your welfare
- You feel cherished and valued as a person
- Responds appropriately and empathically much of the time
- Enjoys your company and taking part in your interests
- Self-supporting, or is working on a realistic plan to become self-supporting
- Is multidimensional—has many interests and activities

This set of characteristics is based on your observations of someone's actions as well as the feelings generated in you when you are with him/her or think about him/her.

Appropriately gives and receives affection can be hard to describe, but whatever the gesture of affection is shown should demonstrate the following:

- Genuineness of feeling, not showing off, or exerting control
- Respect for the receivers worth and value
- An awareness of the environment, and of others in it
- Restraint, prudence, and courtesy
- Confined to appropriate public gestures

Use of affection to show off, to show ownership, and other such motives are not helpful for relationships, and should be seen for what they are.

Attending to you shows interest, caring, concern, and warmth when these actions don't smother, overwhelm you, or are used for power and control. Positive attending means listening and responding, engaging in dialogue, responsiveness to your moods with understanding, and checking with you occasionally to see how you are doing. The negative side is that too much attention is confining, and cuts you off from interactions with others. The lack of attending or sporadic attending shows disinterest and indifference.

Interest in you and your welfare can be very appealing. This interest is shown through the attending previously described, remembering over time what you said that was important for you, trying to understand why you feel and react as you do, showing sensitivity to your moods and feelings, and choosing to be in your company. Again, the positive side is evident, but too much of these behaviors can be negative. Probing and/or continual questioning does not necessarily show interest although some think that they do. Intrusive questions are violations of boundaries, and should be avoided. Let you or the person decide on the amount of self-disclosure. There are some people who can feel attacked when asked several or many questions at a time and it is much more helpful to a relationship to not use interrogation techniques.

Feeling cherished and valued is extremely positive for any relationship, and especially so for an intimate relationship. Notice that these feelings are transcendental and inspirational which addresses the uplifting part or nature of the relationship. When someone is cherished and valued he/she is held in high esteem and appreciated. High esteem is conveyed through actions that show respect for the other person as being separate, unique, and special; lack of criticism, blame, disparaging or demeaning comments about him/her; protection from negative acts and their outcomes; and words and acts of appreciation.

Responding appropriately and empathically most of the time is the most you should expect of anyone. It may not be possible to do so all the time as there are times when others have concerns and problems of their own that can distract them from being fully with you at that time. It is not realistic to expect someone to be emotionally present with you all of the time just as you are not with him/her. But it is realistic to expect a suitable lover to be emotionally present and empathically responsive some of the time.

Enjoys your company extends to liking and wanting to take part in some of your interests, and shared positive experiences can help build relationships. Another part of this is the willingness to let you have interests and activities that are yours alone, and you do the same for him/her. You are not joined at the hip, and have to have all the same interest as this can be smothering and signals possible enmeshment.

Self-supporting or has realistic and reasonable plans for becoming so indicates a person who is independent, responsible, and mature. He/she realizes that self-sufficiency is expected of adults, and does not require that he/she be supported by others except under extreme circumstances such as illness or disability. In addition, it may be necessary to say that this support is gained through legal means, through socially sanctioned and socially responsible means such as work or trust funds. There are situations where the person may not be self-supporting at the time that are still acceptable such as attending school or between jobs. Even then, the person has reasonable plans for becoming self-supporting. It is not wise to take up with anyone who has no visible means of support, and/or someone who has no plans for becoming self-supporting and self-sufficient.

Multidimensional. A multidimensional person has many interests and engages in activities that enrich his/her life. He/she is not narrowly focused, can discuss many topics, and is interesting and engaging in conversations because of the variety of interests and activities. This multidimensionality signals a curiosity and zest for living, a desire to know and learn about a multitude of things, and a tendency for continued growth and development. He/she is not static, hidebound, rigid, stuck, and so on, and not being so can add enrichment and enhancement to the relationship. Pay attention to what a potential lover talks about and is willing to listen about as these can signal one dimensionality or multidimensionality. You may want to examine yourself for this characteristic. When you, or someone else, always seem to talk about the following, these may signal a lack of multidimensionality.

- Work, and work related topics
- Family and personal problems
- Sports
- Fashion and personal grooming
- Other people's problems and misfortunes
- How the world mistreats him/her
- Drinking patterns and exploits
- Parties and partying
- Putting something over on someone

A FEW LAST WORDS

Wrapping up, you now have some descriptions for suitable lovers and you can probably think of some more that you would value. You also have some suggestions for building your self that will help you resist the lures of unsuitable lovers that capitalize on your unmet needs and underdevelopment. You can and will do better with choices and decisions about intimate relationships. Some final thoughts follow:

- Value your self and don't compromise your integrity.
- Associate with principled, moral, ethical people.
- Use STAADA frequently until it becomes somewhat automatic.
- Continue to grow and develop your self, and become your ideal person.
- Set your own course and don't allow others to manipulate and exploit you.
- Like your self and behave in a way that conveys this without being smug or superior. You can like others too.
- Respect yourself, and respect others.

BIBLIOGRAPHY

Brown, N. *Whose Life Is It Anyway?* Oakland, CA: New Harbinger Publications, 2002.
———. *Working with the Self-absorbed.* Oakland, CA: New Harbinger Publications, 2002.
———. *Loving the Self-absorbed.* Oakland, CA: New Harbinger Publications, 2003.
———. *Coping with Your Partner's Jealousy.* Oakland, CA: New Harbinger Publications, 2004.
———. *Coping with Infuriating, Mean, Critical People: The Destructive Narcissistic Pattern.* Westport, CT: Praeger, 2006.
Fromm, E. *The Art of Loving.* New York: Harper & Row, 1956.
Hatfield, E., Cacioppo, J., and Rapson, R. *Emotional Contagion.* Paris: Cambridge University Press. 1994.
Johnson, D., and Johnson, F. *Joining Together* (9th ed.). Boston, MA: Allyn & Bacon, 2003.
Jordan, J., Walker, M., and Hartling, L., eds. *The Complexity of Connection.* New York: The Guilford Press, 2004.
Katherine, A. *Boundaries.* New York: Simon & Schuster, 1991.
Phillips, P., and Phillips, J. "Dear Abby." *The Virginian Pilot* (Norfolk, VA), 2007, 7.
Schiraldi, G. and Kerr, M. *The Anger Management Sourcebook.* New York: McGraw-Hill, 2002.
Schultz, W. *Joy.* New York: Grove Press, 1967.
Shostrom, E. *Freedom To Be.* New York: Bantam, 1974.

INDEX

Acceptance, 3, 120–21

Believer, 74–82; deep desires and
needs, 81–82; projection, 80–81;
transference, 80; vulnerabilities,
87
Boundaries, 4–5; emotional triggers,
132–34; fear, 128–30;
overidentification, 125–26;
parental approval, 131–32; saying
no, 126–28; strategies, 124–25;
violations, 98–99, 123–24

Charming and manipulative type,
41–42, 82–88
Concern, 12–13
Criticism, 13
Curious rebel, 104–5; attention,
111–13; attractors, 109–10;
challenge, 110–11; curiosity, 113;
detaching, 114–15; different, 105;
glamour, 109; interests, 106–7;
motives, 117–18; ordinary, 107–9;
positive rebellion, 115–17;
unknown, 106–7

Disappointment, 22
Disillusion, 21–25

Edges, 18–21
Emotional expression, 9
Empathy, 6; lack, 95–96

Encouragement, 10
Excitement and interest, 10–11
Exotic and different type, 43–44
External behavior, 162–64

Feelings, 25; vocabulary enhancement,
102
Fun, 6

Guilt, 88, 121–23

Helper, 45
Hurting and needy type, 39–41;
attraction, 51; identification, 51,
57–58; strategies, 58

Illusion, romantic, 16; tendency, 18
Impoverished self, 99–104; admiration
hungry, 100–1; attention seeking,
99–100; emptiness, 103; shallow
emotions 101–2
Inclusion, 12
Indifference, boundary, 98–99;
exploitation, 97–98; inappropriate
humor, 96–97; lack of empathy,
95–96
Inflated self, 92–95; arrogance, 94–95;
entitlement, 92–93; unique and
special, 94
Inner resources, 158–62
Interpersonal effectiveness, 135–51;
communication, 143–44; listening

Interpersonal effectiveness (*cont.*)
and responding, 144–48; nonverbal,
    135–41; reduce self-absorption,
    148–51

Lures, 27

Mirror, The, 90–104

Nonverbal communication, 135–41;
    physical appearance, 140–41;
    posture, 139; signals, 136,
    141–43

Resistance, 119–34
Respect, 3, 4
Responsibility, 6
Risk taking and rebellious type, 41,
    70–71; identification, 70
Romance, 17

Saver, 60; association, 69; excitement,
    61; safe and secure, 67
Self-absorbed type, 42–43
Self-absorption, assessment, 148–49;
    behavioral signs, 150; reduction
    strategies, 149–50
Separateness, 13
Shame, 88, 122–24
Sorrow, 25–28
STAADA, 152–56; delay strategies,
    156–58
Susceptibility, 119–34

Termination, 25–28
Trust, 8

Unsuitability: attitudes, 32–33;
    behaviors, 30–31; hidden acts,
    31–32; scale, 33–34; signs,
    29–30; types, 39–44

About the Author

NINA W. BROWN is professor and eminent scholar of counseling at Old Dominion University in Norfolk, Virginia. She is a licensed professional counselor, a nationally certified counselor, and a fellow of the American Group Psychotherapy Association. She obtained her doctorate in counseling from The College of William and Mary, and is the author of seventeen published books, including *Coping with Infuriating, Mean, Critical People* (Praeger, 2006) and *The Unfolding Life* (Praeger, 2003). She can be reached at nbrown@odu.edu.